General edit[illegible]

Brodie's Note[illegible]iam Shakespeare's

Henry IV Part 2

A. J. P. Smith BA (Oxon)
English Department, Kingswood School, Bath

Pan Books London and Sydney

First published 1986 by Pan Books Ltd,
Cavaye Place, London SW10 9PG
9 8 7 6 5 4 3 2 1

ISBN 0 330 50225 5
Photoset by Parker Typesetting Service, Leicester
Printed and bound in Great Britain by
Richard Clay (The Chaucer Press) Ltd, Bungay, Suffolk

Other titles by A. J. P. Smith in the Brodie's Notes series:
Richard II
Measure for Measure
Henry IV Part 1

Contents

Line references in these Notes are to the *Arden Shakespeare: Henry IV Part 2*, but as references are also given to particular acts and scenes, the Notes may be used with any edition of the play.

Preface

This student revision aid is based on the principle that in any close examination of Shakespeare's plays 'the text's the thing'. Seeing a performance, or listening to a tape or record of a performance, is essential and is in itself a valuable and stimulating experience in understanding and appreciation. However, a real evaluation of Shakespeare's greatness, of his universality and of the nature of his literary and dramatic art, can only be achieved by constant application to the texts of the plays themselves. These revised editions of Brodie's Notes are intended to supplement that process through detailed critical commentary.

The first aim of each book is to fix the whole play in the reader's mind by providing a concise summary of the plot, relating it back, where appropriate, to its source or sources. Subsequently the book provides a summary of each scene, followed by *critical comments*. These may convey its importance in the dramatic structure of the play, creation of atmosphere, indication of character development, significance of figurative language etc, and they will also explain or paraphrase difficult words or phrases and identify meaningful references. At the end of each act revision questions are set to test the student's specific and broad understanding and appreciation of the play.

An extended critical commentary follows this scene by scene analysis. This embraces such major elements as characterization, imagery, the use of blank verse and prose, soliloquies and other aspects of the play which the editor considers need close attention. The paramount aim is to send the reader back to the text. The book concludes with a series of revision questions which require a detailed knowledge of the play; the first of these has notes by the editor of what *might* be included in a written answer. The intention is to stimulate and to guide; the whole emphasis of this commentary is to encourage the student's *involvement* in the play, to develop disciplined critical responses and thus promote personal enrichment through the imaginative experience of our greatest writer.

Graham Handley

Shakespeare and the Elizabethan playhouse

William Shakespeare was born in Stratford-upon-Avon in 1564, and there are reasons to suppose that he came from a relatively prosperous family. He was probably educated at Stratford Grammar School and, at the age of eighteen, married Anne Hathaway, who was twenty-six. They had three children, a girl born shortly after their marriage, followed by twins in 1585 (the boy died in 1596). It seems likely that Shakespeare left for London shortly after a company of travelling players had visited Stratford in 1585, for by 1592 – according to the jealous testimony of one of his fellow-writers Robert Greene – he was certainly making his way both as actor and dramatist. The theatres were closed because of the plague in 1593; when they reopened Shakespeare worked with the Lord Chamberlain's Men, later the King's Men, and became a shareholder in each of the two theatres with which he was most closely associated, the Globe and the Blackfriars. He later purchased New Place, a considerable property in his home town of Stratford, to which he retired in 1611; there he entertained his great contemporary Ben Jonson (1572–1637) and the poet Michael Drayton (1563–1631). An astute businessman, Shakespeare lived comfortably in the town until his death in 1616.

This is a very brief outline of the life of our greatest writer, for little more can be said of him with certainty, though the plays – and poems – are living witness to the wisdom, humanity and many-faceted nature of the man. He was both popular and successful as a dramatist, perhaps less so as an actor. He probably began work as a dramatist in the late 1580s, by collaborating with other playwrights and adapting old plays, and by 1598 Francis Meres was paying tribute to his excellence in both comedy and tragedy. His first original play was probably *Love's Labour's Lost* (1590) and while the theatres were closed during the plague he wrote his narrative poems *Venus and Adonis* (1593) and *The Rape of Lucrece* (1594). The sonnets were almost certainly written in the 1590s though not published until 1609; the first 126 are addressed to a young man who was his friend and patron, while the rest are concerned with the 'dark lady'.

The dating of Shakespeare's plays has exercised scholars ever since the publication of the First Folio (1623), which listed them as comedies, histories and tragedies. It seems more important to look at them chronologically as far as possible, in order to trace Shakespeare's considerable development as a dramatist. The first period, say to the middle of the 1590s, included such plays as *Love's Labour's Lost, The Comedy of Errors, Richard III, The Taming of the Shrew, Romeo and Juliet* and *Richard II*. These early plays embrace the categories listed in the First Folio, so that Shakespeare the craftsman is evident in his capacity for variety of subject and treatment. The next phase includes *A Midsummer Night's Dream, The Merchant of Venice, Henry IV Parts 1 and 2, Henry V* and *Much Ado About Nothing*, as well as *Julius Caesar, As You Like It* and *Twelfth Night*. These are followed, in the early years of the century, by his great tragic period: *Hamlet, Othello, King Lear* and *Macbeth*, with *Antony and Cleopatra* and *Coriolanus* belonging to 1607–09. The final phase embraces the romances (1610–13), *Cymbeline, The Tempest* and *The Winter's Tale* and the historical play *Henry VIII*.

Each of these revision aids will place the individual text under examination in the chronology of the remarkable dramatic output that spanned twenty years from the early 1590s to about 1613. The practical theatre for which Shakespeare wrote and acted derived from the inn courtyards in which performances had taken place, the few playhouses in his day being modelled on their structure. They were circular or hexagonal in shape, allowing the balconies and boxes around the walls full view of the stage. This large stage, which had no scenery, jutted out into the pit, the most extensive part of the theatre, where the poorer people – the 'groundlings' – stood. There was no roof (though the Blackfriars, used from 1608 onwards, was an indoor theatre) and thus bad weather meant no performance. Certain plays were acted at court, and these private performances normally marked some special occasion. Costumes, often rich ones, were used, and music was a common feature, with musicians on or under the stage; this sometimes had additional features, for example a trapdoor to facilitate the entry of a ghost. Women were barred by law from appearing on stage, and all female parts were played by boy actors; this undoubtedly explains the many instances in Shakespeare where a woman has to conceal her identity by disguising

herself as a man, e.g. Rosalind in *As You Like It*, Viola in *Twelfth Night*.

Shakespeare and his contemporaries often adapted their plays from sources in history and literature, extending an incident or a myth or creating a dramatic narrative from known facts. They were always aware of their own audiences, and frequently included topical references, sometimes of a satirical flavour, which would appeal to – and be understood by – the groundlings as well as their wealthier patrons who occupied the boxes. Shakespeare obviously learned much from his fellow dramatists and actors, being on good terms with many of them. Ben Jonson paid generous tribute to him in the lines prefaced to the First Folio of Shakespeare's plays:

Thou art a monument without a tomb,
And art alive still, while thy book doth live
And we have wits to read, and praise to give.

Among his contemporaries were Thomas Kyd (1558–94) and Christopher Marlowe (1564–93). Kyd wrote *The Spanish Tragedy*, the revenge motif here foreshadowing the much more sophisticated treatment evident in *Hamlet*, while Marlowe evolved the 'mighty line' of blank verse, a combination of natural speech and elevated poetry. The quality and variety of Shakespeare's blank verse owes something to the innovatory brilliance of Marlowe but carries the stamp of individuality, richness of association, technical virtuosity and, above all, the genius of imaginative power.

The texts of Shakespeare's plays are still rich sources for scholars, and the editors of these revision aids have used the Arden editions of Shakespeare, which are regarded as preeminent for their scholarly approach. They are strongly recommended for advanced students, but other editions, like the New Penguin Shakespeare, the New Swan, the Signet are all good annotated editions currently available. A reading list of selected reliable works on the play being studied is provided at the end of each commentary and students are advised to turn to these as their interest in the play deepens.

Literary terms used in these notes

Anachronism An occurrence, or artefact in an inappropriate time-setting.
Blank verse Unrhymed verse in ten-syllable lines.
Climax A crucial moment, of high emotional charge, it usually occurs just before the resolution of the drama. Increasing tension precedes climax.
Dramatic irony This occurs in a play when a character speaks words the full significance of which he does not realize. The audience, assuming that it is in full possession of the facts, *does* appreciate the significance of the character's words.
Imagery Any figurative use of language. Often 'word-pictures', which utilize the capacity of the mind to respond emotionally to an idea which is being evoked by the words.
Irony This occurs when the real meaning of what is expressed is at variance with what appears to be said, i.e. the surface meaning is in conflict with what is really meant.
Malapropism Derived from Mrs Malaprop in Sheridan's play *The Rivals* (1775). She confused similar sounding words just as The Hostess does in Act II Scene 1.
Metaphor A comparison which is unequivocally implied or expressed, without the use of 'like' or 'as'.
Pathos This occurs when a piece of writing evokes pity.
Rhythm Language has a natural distribution of sound-emphasis, sometimes called 'stress' or 'rhythm.' When the stresses occur regularly, it is called 'metre'.
Pun A play on words, which exploits the fact that words of the same sound may have more than one meaning.
Simile A figure of speech, introduced by 'like' or 'as', which compares two essentially dissimilar things.

The play
Plot and structure

Plot

Henry IV Part 2 continues the story of *Henry IV Part 1*, with substantially the same characters. The King has won the battle of Shrewsbury, but there are still other conspirators under arms, notably the Archbishop of York and the Earl of Northumberland. The main plot of the play deals with events leading to the defeat of the Archibishop of York by the trickery of Prince John of Lancaster, the King's third son, in Gaultree Forest, Yorkshire. Later, we learn of the defeat of the Earl of Northumberland by the Sheriff of Yorkshire, though this is not shown on the stage. In the hour of success the King dies, but not before a reconciliation with his wayward son and heir, the young Prince Henry, who has caused him so much concern. Whereas everyone now thinks that England will go to rack and ruin under the riotous young Prince, he very soon shows that he has every intention of ruling the country effectively and justly.

There are some lively scenes of low-life, the heart and soul of which is a fat knight, Sir John Falstaff, who, up to now, has been the constant companion of the Prince. These scenes make up the sub-plot (or comic plot). Sir John travels to Gloucestershire, on active service for the King, but he uses his commission to make money for himself, and carefully arranges things so that he arrives too late to do any serious fighting, though he does make an important capture. After an all-night ride, he arrives back in London just in time to see the new King at his coronation. He expects to be much honoured now that his friend is King. Instead, he is summarily dismissed and sent to prison, although he is promised a small pension.

Just as the play continues the story of *Henry IV Part 1*, so it looks forward to *Henry V*. The new King dedicates himself to his office, and declares that he has turned away his former self. The last words of the play point to a French campaign within a year; this will become the main action of *Henry V*.

The historical period of the action of *Henry IV Part 2* occupies nearly ten years, from a few days after the battle of Shrewsbury, which took place in 1403, to the coronation day of Henry V, in

1413. Shakespeare 'telescopes' this period of time considerably in his play.

Structure

There are two plots in *Henry IV Part 2*: the main plot is concerned with the rebellion against the King; the 'secondary' plot centres on Falstaff and follows him from London to Gloucestershire and back again to London, where he is rejected by Henry V. Links are forged between the two by the Prince, who obviously has dealings with his father and visits Falstaff in the Boar's Head in order to play a practical joke upon him. Falstaff, apart from his meeting with the new King at his coronation, briefly skirmishes at Gaultree Forest, where the rebels are defeated.

Shakespeare evidently intends us to see many parallels and contrasts in the two plots. Both begin with sick, old men: Northumberland and Falstaff; the King, too, is old and ailing. Thus in the play we are strongly aware that the end of an era is upon us. Falstaff and the rebels obviously represent the disorder which threatens the kingdom, the one operating primarily on a moral level, the other showing us disorder on a political level (as well as moral).

Shakespeare is working with history and thus we cannot expect to feel undue suspense as to the outcome of events, but it is still noteworthy that the play seems almost deliberately to eschew climaxes. The defeat of the rebels (conspicuously a mundane piece of treachery) is very 'flat' and the reconciliation between father and son, whilst it has considerable dramatic and thematic interest, is entirely predictable – and has already, in a sense, occurred in *Henry IV Part 1*. Similarly, the rejection of Falstaff comes as no surprise and merely presents in public form something that has in fact taken place long before.

Sources and treatment, date and setting

Sources and treatment

Shakespeare's main source for the political plot of the play was Holinshed's *Chronicles of England, Scotland and Ireland* which was published in 1577. This work interprets history from a Tudor standpoint and stresses the disastrous consequences for England of the deposition and murder of Richard II by Henry Bolingbroke. It also mentions the reformation of the Prince, but does not suggest any motivation – merely stating that he banished his 'misrulie mates' and forbade them to 'approach, lodge, or sojourne within ten miles of his court or presence'.

In the interests of dramatic presentation, Shakespeare condenses and alters the sequence of Holinshed's rambling narrative, and he gives substance to the characters. There are some interesting divergences from Holinshed; for example, Shakespeare enhances Hal's military career by making him accompany his father on the campaign in Wales – this does not appear in the *Chronicle*. Also, Shakespeare extends Henry IV's illness to cover the whole of the play. Holinshed makes Westmoreland the architect of the treachery which undoes the rebels, whereas Shakespeare implicates Prince John much more clearly. Northumberland is presented as treacherous and almost entirely villainous in Shakespeare, whereas Holinshed is not concerned to blacken him.

Some of the tone of the play derives from Samuel Daniel's *The First Fowre Bookes of the Ciuille Wars Between the Two Houses of Lancaster and Yorke* (1595), although it is notable that Shakespeare presents Henry IV as seeking to cling to power, whereas Daniel relates that he sought to abdicate. Shakespeare also drew upon Stow's *Annals of England* and *Chronicles of England* (1580).

The origin of the low-life scenes would seem to be a play which had enjoyed some popularity, called *The Famous Victories of Henry V*. This crude work exploited the legend of Hal's youthful wildness, dramatizing in episodic fashion, his riotous behaviour and loose-living friends – one of whom was named Jockey Oldcastle, a name which was later changed by Shakespeare to 'Falstaff' in order not to give offence to Oldcastle's descendants (vide 'The Epilogue'). In this play we find, in embryonic form, the crown-on-the-pillow episode.

Date

The text of the play was purchased in 1600 from the Lord Chamberlain's Men (Shakespeare's theatre company) by the publishers Andrew Wise and William Aspley. Later in the year the play was published in Quarto form. There is no other Quarto edition extant (cf. *Henry IV Part 1*, which exists in six Quarto editions). *Part 2* next appears in the First Folio edition of 1623.

Setting

The play deals with the last ten years of Henry IV's reign. Shakespeare is not concerned to give his play a 'period flavour' – it would have been acted in the dress of his day and such references to local colour as we find relate to Elizabethan times rather than the early fifteenth century. Hence the various anachronisms such as references to a 'caliver' and the drills which may be performed with it. The places in London which are described or are evoked are essentially Elizabethan, as is the obsession with venereal disease – a frequent topic of the times. Constables and beadles are thoroughly Elizabethan. The Gloucestershire scenes in particular give us the essence of the country life in and around Stratford-on-Avon, where Shakespeare grew up.

Scene summaries, critical commentaries, textual notes and revision questions

Induction

The Induction indicates to the audience the point at which Shakespeare intends to take up the story again. We are to deal with the events contingent upon the King's victory at Shrewsbury.

The tenor of Rumour's speech introduces an atmosphere of turmoil and uncertainty and stresses the necessity to face uncomfortable truths rather than take refuge behind 'smooth comforts false'.

Rumour . . . tongues A traditional personification. Commonly portrayed as wearing a garment upon which tongues were painted.
vent of hearing The ears.
drooping Refers to the setting sun.
post-horse A horse kept at an inn upon which a traveller could continue his journey.
still Always.
Make . . . musters Cause armies to be mustered in preparation for an anticipated invasion.
big Made pregnant with.
And no such matter Whereas in reality such apprehensions are groundless.
jealousies Suspicions.
plain a stop So easy to play.
blunt monster i.e. the dull-witted multitude.
my household Refers to the audience. We are all 'close relatives' of Rumour.
But what . . . at first Rumour rebukes itself for uncharacteristically speaking truthfully.
To noise abroad Rumour has spread this false report of the Battle of Shrewsbury.
Harry Monmouth Prince Henry.
worm-eaten . . . ragged stone i.e. Northumberland's dilapidated castle.
crafty-sick Northumberland is pretending to be sick – possibly to arouse the sympathy of the victorious King, as well as to account for his non-appearance at Shrewsbury.
tiring on Riding on to the point of exhaustion.
smooth . . . false i.e. false reassurances.
true wrongs Implies that it is much the worse course to disguise evil tidings.

Act I Scene 1

Lord Bardolph brings the Earl of Northumberland a false report about the outcome of the Battle of Shrewsbury. Apparently, Northumberland has been feigning sickness, hence he was unable to attend the battle in person. Lord Bardolph's fallacious account of the rebels' victory is shortly succeeded by an account from Travers of the rebels' defeat and the death of Northumberland's son, Hotspur. Northumberland is confused, not knowing whom to believe. The doleful appearance of Morton, together with his version of the battle, convinces the Earl that his faction has suffered a calamitous defeat and that his son is dead.

Northumberland indulges in a fit of passion but he is soon pacified by the assurances of Morton that all is not lost. The Archbishop of York is leading another conspiracy against Henry IV. Northumberland is led to believe that the chances of the success of this rebellion are enhanced by the spiritual authority of the Archbishop.

Commentary

The note of confusion and turmoil which was apparent in Rumour's speech is given vivid life by this scene. The conflicting versions of the outcome of the battle introduce an immediate atmosphere of uncertainty. The intemperate fury of Northumberland, in which he invokes the spirit of Cain upon the land, may be impotent but it is certainly threatening. Even more ominous is the knowledge that the Archbishop is leading a further rebellion against the King.

Clearly, England is about to suffer further discord. Shakespeare reminds us that the origin of these troubles may be located in the murder of the anointed king, Richard II at Pomfret Castle. This murder was instigated by Henry Bolingbroke, who now occupies the throne in the person of Henry IV. At the time of Richard's murder, Northumberland was Bolingbroke's accomplice. The result of Richard's murder, as Shakespeare revealed in the earlier plays, *Richard II* and *Henry IV, Part 1*, was a period of bloody civil strife – former alliances disintegrated: Northumberland, feeling himself slighted by Bolingbroke, ranged himself against the King. The defeat of the rebel faction at Shrewsbury might have ended the turmoil, but Shakespeare, in this scene, shows us that this is not to be.

stratagem Act of violence.
The times . . . wild Reinforces the theme of Rumour's speech.
contention Strife.
high feeding Fed on too rich a diet.
brawn Fattened boar.
dignify the times Give honour to our age.
over-rode Out-rode.
haply Perhaps.
turned me back Met with me and sent me back to you.
forspent Exhausted.
jade Nag.
rowel-headed Part of a spur.
again Say to me again.
point Lace used for holding up hose.
hilding Base.
spoke . . . venture Only guessed.
strond Shore.
priam King of Troy at the time when it was sacked.
but priam . . . tongue But Priam realized that Troy was on fire before the messenger could bring himself to speak of it.
to stop . . . indeed To prevent me from ever exercising my powers of hearing again.
is chanced Has come to pass.
divination Suspicion.
gainsaid Contradicted.
strange Reluctant.
quittance Exchange of blows.
bruited Reported.
best-temper'd i.e. those of strongest character.
metal The imagery in this passage is drawn from 'tempering' steel. There is also a pun on the word 'mettle', meaning fighting spirit.
abated Grown blunt.
Turn'd . . . lead The imagery here likens the soldiers' losing heart to the edge of a sword losing sharpness – as if the sword itself was composed of lead.
well-labouring Labouring to good purpose.
three times . . . King Douglas had killed three counterfeit kings in the battle at Shrewsbury.
vail his stomach Lose heart for the fight.
grace . . . backs The flight of Douglas gave an apparent 'grace' to the running away of the rebel soldiers.
at full In full.
physic Medicine.
made me well Paradoxically, Northumberland proclaims himself cured of his sickness by this bad news.
buckle under life i.e. are not fit to bear the weight of a living man.
keeper's arms i.e. the arms of the person who is nursing him.

nice Unmanly.
scaly gauntlet i.e. composed of 'scale-armour'.
coif Night-cap.
wanton Effeminate.
flesh'd with conquest The conquerors, having tasted the flesh of conquest, are now lusting for more.
with iron i.e. a helmet.
ragged'st Roughest.
Let . . . earth i.e. let there be a time of total confusion.
flood The seas.
ling'ring act A protracted struggle.
Cain The first murderer, according to Genesis. Significantly, in this context, Cain murdered his brother, Abel. In this speech, Northumberland invites a time of disorder and bloodshed – particularly shocking to an Elizabethan audience: they would have viewed the prospect of internecine strife with great horror.
rude Violent.
cast th'event Calculated the outcome.
the account of chance The possibilities inherent in success or failure.
make head Raise an army.
dole of blows The dealing out of blows.
capable Vulnerable.
forward Eager.
trade of danger i.e. where he was most likely to find danger.
this i.e. risks and dangers.
stiff-borne Obstinately pursued (action).
wrought out life Came through it with our lives intact.
ten to one i.e. the chances were ten to one against us.
Choked Disregarded.
o'erset Defeated.
put forth A pun: set forth on another similar voyage; stake everything again.
up i.e. up in armed revolt.
double surety i.e. having both spiritual and temporal authority.
potions Medicines.
Turns . . . religion Gives spiritual authority to the name of rebellion.
Pomfret The castle in which Richard II was murdered.
bestride Stands over protectively.
more and less The mighty and the humble.
posts Messengers.
so few i.e. they have few friends.

Act I Scene 2

Falstaff enters, accompanied by his diminutive page. Falstaff feels unwell (he has consulted a doctor) and his credit-worthiness has evaporated. Reluctantly, he comes face to face with the Lord Chief Justice, who is prepared to overlook his past crime because of Falstaff's apparent valour at the Battle of Shrewsbury. The audience, of course, would be aware that it had no basis in fact – Falstaff was entirely cowardly in battle. The Chief Justice sternly rebukes Falstaff, in particular for his misleading of the young Prince Hal; also, he is unmoved by Falstaff's attempts at self-justification and at presenting himself as being young and vigorous. There is a deep antipathy between them.

We learn that Falstaff has been ordered to go with Prince John of Lancaster against the army of Northumberland and the Archbishop of York. The prospect does not delight Falstaff, who attributes this posting to the intervention of the Chief Justice.

Commentary

The first appearance of Falstaff links him with the rebel leader, Northumberland: they are both old, sick men. They live in the past. Falstaff, as we shall see, cherishes the unfounded belief that his relationship with Prince Hal is still firm and believes that he will undoubtedly be granted a position of significance when Hal becomes king. In fact, as a reading of *Henry IV Part 1* reveals, this has never been a serious possibility.

Falstaff enters, ironically, at the height of his prestige: he has earned an entirely spurious reputation as the slayer of the rebel leader, Hotspur. This deed was, in reality, performed by Hal. Shakespeare underlines the ludicrousness of Falstaff's heroism by giving him a mock-triumphal entry – attended by a minute pageboy.

To some extent we see a familiar Falstaff; all the old poses are evident, as they were in *Henry IV Part 1*: he pretends to be youthful, he attempts to exploit petty tradesmen and to portray himself essentially as virtuous and misunderstood. On this occasion, however, his wiles fall upon the deaf ears of the Lord Chief Justice, who is not disposed to enter into any banter with him, and has an unflinching grasp of the realities of Falstaff's character. If we set alongside the remarks of the Chief Justice – and the facts that Falstaff's credit-worthiness no longer exists and that he is apparently ailing – then it is impossible to escape the conclusion that reality is catching up with Falstaff.

buckler A small, round shield.
giant An ironic reference to the page's small stature.
water Urine. Used diagnostically by doctors.
party Person.
owed Owned.
gird Ridicule.
foolish-compounded Composed of follies.
invented on me Falstaff sees himself as the source of all laughter.
set me off i.e. make Falstaff appear ridiculous, because he is attended by so tiny a servant.
mandrake A plant which, because of its forked root, was thought to resemble a man.
manned with an agate Possessed for a servant a person no bigger than an agate stone. Agate stones were customarily ring stones: often they were carved into small human shapes.
juvenal The youth.
face-royal An elaborate pun which depends upon the King possessing a kingly face and that his image would appear on the ten-shilling coin (a royal). In the latter sense, the face would not require the attentions of a barber.
finish it i.e. 'complete' it (by adding a beard).
not a hair amiss i.e. not blemished by one hair.
He may . . . of it He may keep it at its 'face-value' (i.e. full value) – he will not have to spend so much as sixpence on having a shave.
crowing Boasting (that he may be termed a man).
grace Title and estimation.
slops Wide, fashionable breeches.
assurance Surety.
glutton . . . hotter A reference to the story of Dives and Lazarus. Dives, tormented by the fires of hell, sent to Lazarus for water. See Luke, 16, 24.
Achitophel The betrayer of Absolom (2 Samuel, 15, 12).
yea-forsooth knave A rascal given to swearing feeble oaths.
to bear . . . hand Deceive.
smooth-pates i.e. a short, fashionable hairstyle.
high shoes . . . keys Indicative of pride and possessions.
through Thorough.
taking up Obtaining purchases on credit.
stand . . . security Demand security.
lief Gladly.
ratsbane A poison.
horn Refers to the 'horn of plenty' – cornucopia.
lightness Infidelity. Cuckolds were supposed to grow horns on their heads.
lanthorn Lantern (the light shone through panels of horn).
Paul's St Paul's in London, where servants might be hired.
committed i.e. to prison . . . An allusion to the legend that Hal was

committed to prison for striking the Lord Chief Justice.
charge Commission to raise soldiers.
hunt counter i.e. to hunt after the wrong scent.
advice In accordance with your doctor's advice.
age Another pun: ague=age.
saltness This remark is ambiguous: Falstaff implies that his persecutor is 'salt' in the sense of youthful; or old, requiring salt to act as a preservative.
apoplexy Paralysis.
Galen A Greek physician (AD 130–200?).
by the heels i.e. in the stocks.
Job Old Testament figure, legendary for his power to endure suffering. See Job, 1–2.
the wise . . . scruple Even a wise man may be permitted to doubt.
land-service Falstaff puns on his military service, which he believes will be a defence against the accusation of his robbery at Gad's Hill. Military service would render him immune from prosecution.
the fellow with the great belly Possibly a topical allusion to a famous beggar whose belly was so great that he required a dog to lead him.
gall Make more paintful.
Gad's Hill See *Henry IV Part 1, II, 2.*
o'erposting Overlooking.
To wake . . . fox Another form of the proverb 'Let sleeping dogs lie!'
wassail candle A festive, long-lasting candle.
wax A pun on 'wax', meaning to grow big.
gravity i.e. the seriousness of manner appropriate to the elderly.
gravy An obvious pun on 'gravity' – in this instance Falstaff refers to his grease-stained beard.
ill angel In this case, 'evil spirit'.
ill angel is light A reference to the illegal practice of coin-clipping. (An angel=10 shillings).
I cannot go A pun: 'I cannot walk' and 'I cannot pass as good currency'.
costermongers' times i.e. times when nothing is valuable if it does not make a profit. Costermongers (originally apple-sellers) were synonymous with hucksters.
bearherd Bear-keeper. Valour only finds an outlet in exhibiting wild animals.
pregnancy Quick-wittedness.
reckonings Tavern bills.
malice . . . shapes them Owing to the direction given to them by these present times.
livers The seat of the passions.
galls Bitterness. Falstaff implies that the Lord Chief Justice has allowed himself to become soured with age. Ludicrously, Falstaff still considers himself to be youthful.
vaward The vanguard, the forefront

wags i.e. full of jests.
written down Obviously bear the signs of.
wit single Intellectually feeble.
hallooing A pun: making hallowed utterances and hallooing to hounds.
anthems Sacred songs.
caper Dance. Falstaff goes on to offer himself as a contestant in a dancing competition.
rude Crude.
sensible Reasonable.
checked Rebuked.
ashes and sackcloth The signs of penitence.
sack A sweet white wine, much beloved by Falstaff.
severed Parted.
I thank, etc. Falstaff attributes this unwelcome military service to the malicious influence of the Lord Chief Justice.
look you Make sure that you.
kiss . . . at home i.e. all of you that enjoy a peaceful life at home.
our armies . . . hot day Implies that if it is too hot for Falstaff to fight, then those who remain at home cannot expect to enjoy the blessings of peace for very long.
I might . . . white To be able to 'spit white' was apparently a sign of good health, but the precise reference is obscure.
crosses A pun: 'troubles' and money stamped with a cross.
fillip . . . beetle i.e. cause me to be thrown (flipped) by a battering ram.
degrees Stages in life.
prevent Come before.
groats An insignificant amount of money.
mistress Ursula i.e. the Hostess, Mistress Quickly.
halt Limp.
colour Pretext.
commodity Self-interest.

Act I Scene 3

The rebel leaders assess their position. They have doubts about the powers of Northumberland. Lord Bardolph is noticeably more cautious than Hastings and reminds him of the follies of Hotspur, who came to grief because his expectations did not match up to the reality of the military situation. Some comfort is drawn from the knowledge that the King is already occupied with the Welsh and the French. The Archbishop urges the enterprise forward, and makes some generalizations about the fickleness of the mob.

Commentary

The rebels are not presented in a favourable light: the Archbishop whom we were led to believe 'turns insurrection to religion' is allegedly concerned to avenge the usurpation of Richard II, but here, and later, it appears that he is more motivated by a personal detestation of Bolingbroke. He does not strike one as a godly man. Northumberland is said to be motivated by revenge. Mowbray and the others are evidently concerned to take advantage of the troubled times to right their own sense of grievance and to pursue self-aggrandizement. Less time is spent talking about their cause than is devoted to their debating their chances of success. The division of the King's forces is a point in their favour, but they are cautious and unsure of themselves. The Archbishop's remarks about the mob have some justification but his words could equally apply to himself and the whole rebel faction. It is far from clear why they should imagine that they will be more successful on this occasion than they were at the Battle of Shrewsbury.

allow the occasion Grant the justification of our cause.
puissance Power.
grow upon the file Now total, amount to.
supplies Reinforcements.
May hold up head May stand confidently.
by the hand Close at hand.
theme Undertaking.
Eating . . . supply Feeding himself on illusions and the mere promise of reinforcements.
Flatt' ring . . . thoughts Deceiving himself into believing that he would receive reinforcements, which turned out to be fewer in number than his most pessimistic estimate.
winking With his eyes closed, blindly.
To lay down . . . of hope To investigate the possibilities of what may be hoped for.
Yes . . . them Very obscure lines about which there is much disagreement. The general sense seems to be that it does do harm if, in a state of imminent war, the hopes which are entertained are like those we anticipate at the outset of spring at the mere sight of buds. These hopes frequently turn out to be false and fruit is often blighted by the frost. The caution is against false optimism.
outweighs ability Is beyond our means.
offices Rooms.
Consent . . . foundation Agree after having taken appropriate deliberations.

estate Means.
his opposite i.e. those factors which are against the undertaking.
Gives o'er Gives up.
part-created cost The creation, expensive, yet half-built.
subject Object.
waste A wastefully created edifice – prone to the depradations of winter.
and that . . . expectation And that we are now possessed of every single man that we can hope for.
heads Forces.
several Various.
commonwealth Nation.
fond Foolish (multitude).
Bolingbroke/Richard this passage reminds us of recent history and of Shakespeare's *Richard II* and *Henry IV Part 1*. Richard was originally fêted by the populace, who later rejected him and granted their favours to Bolingbroke. Thus Bolingbroke was able to mount the throne as Henry IV – having usurped the throne from Richard and had him murdered. The fickleness of the mob is an abiding theme in Shakespeare.
trimm'd Decked out.
beastly Bestial, like an animal.
glutton Gluttonous. The imagery is of a greedy hound which devours its food so readily that it becomes sick.
vomit Echo of Proverbs, 26 11ff.
Thou i.e. the multitude.
draw our numbers Assemble our forces.

Revision questions on Act I

1 Discuss the main themes of Rumour's speech.

2 What impression does Northumberland make upon you?

3 With examples, show who wins 'the duel of wit' between the Chief Justice and Falstaff.

4 What weaknesses are apparent in the rebel faction?

5 Does the scene with Falstaff bear any thematic relationship with the other scenes of the Act?

Act II Scene 1

This is set in a tavern in Eastcheap – a familiar haunt of Falstaff. We learn that Mistress Quickly, the Hostess, has arranged for Falstaff's arrest. He is accused of breach of promise and not paying his debts – on both counts the Hostess is the aggrieved party. Falstaff and his page easily discountenance the arresting officers, but the ensuing brawl is interrupted by the arrival of the Lord Chief Justice. Falstaff's attempts to plead innocence are to no avail, and he is ordered to make due restitution to the Hostess. Gower arrives with the news that the King is returning to London, which indicates the seriousness of the threat posed by the rebellion. Falstaff is required to proceed to York, but first he invites Gower to dinner. The invitation is declined. With a final rebuke, the Lord Chief Justice departs.

Commentary

The scene opens on a note of knockabout farce: at the request of the Hostess, Fang (the bailiff) and two officers seek to arrest Falstaff. The Hostess is a foolish, good-hearted woman who has been mercilessly exploited by Sir John; she endearingly muddles up her words and proclaims herself to have been eaten out of house and home. Falstaff, in order to escape paying his debts, has promised to marry her – a promise he never intends to fulfil. Underlying the fun, however, there is a more serious note: we should not allow ourselves to be blinded to the fact that Falstaff has behaved badly, and this is particularly apparent when he dismisses the Hostess as a madwoman, in front of the Lord Chief Justice.

Of course, the Chief Justice is not taken in and no amount of bluster can save Falstaff from his stern rebuke: 'Sir John, I am well acquainted with your manner of wrenching the true cause the false way.' In *Henry IV Part 1*, the Prince had frequently pointed out the follies of Falstaff; here, this function is taken on by the Chief Justice. In the former play, Falstaff had been allowed to escape with his follies and self-respect; in this play we note that the Chief Justice is relentless in his opposition to all that Falstaff stands for – his parting shot ('thou art a great fool') is unequivocal, and Falstaff is not granted the privilege of a reply. Also, we note that his question 'What's the news my lords?' is blatantly ignored: Falstaff is treated as an irrelevancy when there is real business to be discussed.

yeoman Bailiff's man.
Will stand to't? Will he go through with it?

stabbed Obviously carries a bawdy, sexual second meaning.
foin Thrust.
infinitive . . . score Malapropism (the misuse of a word through similarity of sound). The Hostess means that Falstaff is infinitely in her debt.
continuantly Another malapropism: mixing up continually with incontinently.
Pie Corner A street in London.
saving Excusing.
indited 'Invited'.
Lubber's Head The 'Lippard's (Leopard's) Head' – an inn.
Lumbert Lombard.
exion Action.
long one Major debt.
borne Endured. Also carries a bawdy second meaning.
unless . . . wrong Unless women were made to endure men's wrongs – like beasts of burden. Again, a bawdy second meaning.
malmsey-mose i.e. red-nosed, through drinking of malmsey (a wine).
Whose . . . dead? What's all the fuss about?
quean A pejorative term for a woman: 'hussy'.
channel Gutter.
bastardly Dastardly.
honeysuckle Homicidal.
honeyseed Homicide.
-queller -killer!
hempseed Child destined for 'the hemp' – the hangman's rope.
scullion A term of abuse – 'kitchen drudge'.
rampallion, fustilarian Nonsense words – derogatory of Mistress Quickly.
catastrophe 'Nether regions'.
stand to Stand by me.
mare Possibly a nightmare. Falstaff takes 'mare' in a more obvious, sexual sense.
vantage of ground to get up Another sexual allusion as well as the sense 'had I the advantage of high ground so that I could mount a mare'.
by her own By what is rightfully hers.
parcel-gilt Partly gilt.
Wheeson Whitsun.
gossip Friend, confidant.
mess A quantity of.
green i.e. not yet healed.
book oath Bible oath.
distracted Made her mad.
level True.
practised Deceived.
sterling . . . current A monetary witticism.

sneap Rebuke.
as having power to do wrong As if you had licence to behave villainously.
in the effect of In accordance with.
I . . . fain I shall be obliged to.
glasses . . . drinking 'Glasses' are nowadays the fashionable drinking-vessels.
the Prodigal A common allegorical decoration for wall-tapestries. See Luke, 15, 11–32.
waterwork Painted walls (instead of tapestries).
bed-hangers Bed-curtains.
humours Fits of bad temper.
draw Withdraw from.
Hook on The sincerity of Falstaff's promises may be judged by this contemptuous aside.
presently Immediately.
tap for tap Hit for hit. Falstaff regards his dealings with the Chief Justice as a fencing-match.
lighten A pun: make you lighter (in terms of weight); also, 'enlighten'.

Act II Scene 2

A bored and disconsolate Prince, in conversation with Poins, is interrupted by the arrival of Bardolph and the Page. A letter, written in a very flowery style, is presented to Hal – it brings greetings from Falstaff, together with a warning that Hal should not put too much faith in Poins. The Prince, on hearing that Falstaff is to dine at the Boar's Head tavern, hatches a plot which will cause Falstaff to reveal himself in his true colours. As yet, the details of the scheme are obscure, but it is to involve Hal and Poins disguising themselves as waiters and attending at Falstaff's table.

Commentary

The Prince's first words are significant: he appears weighed-down by some not very clearly defined malaise. He is obviously uneasy about his style of life. We need to remember that he has recently killed Hotspur and become reunited with his father. Yet he finds himself consorting with the old gang in Eastcheap. Falstaff may think (or hope) that nothing has changed, but it is immediately obvious that the Prince is not the young man he was in *Henry IV Part 1*. It is tempting to conjecture that he is genuinely disturbed by his father's ill-health and that he perhaps senses the proximity of his own kingship – with all its attendant anxieties and responsibilities. There is something laboured about his jesting with Poins, and his scheme to discountenance Falstaff (yet again) is undertaken in an almost perfunctory manner. Hal agrees to participate with none of the *joie de vivre* which he displayed when plotting the Gad's Hill episode in the earlier play.

By now the mood of the play may be clearly perceived. It is downbeat: we saw this first of all in the presentation of Falstaff, who is ailing, and irrelevant to the powerful characters in the play; he is also rather more unpleasant – particularly in his dealings with the Hostess. He is no match for the Chief Justice. Hal likewise, as we have seen here, is ill at ease and less eager to play up to the follies of those who surround him.

small beer Weak beer. i.e. trival pursuits, more befitting a child.
loosely studied Lax in what he finds to interest him.
composition Refers to the weak beer.
Belike then In all probability.
bear Have in my mind.
for superfluity As a change.
tennis court keeper . . . racket there Hal implies that so long as Poins has two shirts (one to play in and one to wear) he will be sure to be found wasting his time at the tennis-courts.
the rest of thy low counties, etc. The reminder of this speech exhibits elaborate and obscene punning. 'Low countries', as well as being another name for Holland, means 'nether regions' (sexual parts). Holland is also a name for fine linen. Shift could either mean scheme, change of clothes or the undergarment of a woman. The overall implication is that Poins has been so busy with nether regions that he has begotten many a bastard and been forced to either pawn his fine linen or use it as clothing to wrap his offspring in!
kindreds . . . strengthened Families are caused to multiply.
It shall serve It'll do.
stand the push Stand up to your thrust.
albeit Although.
Very hardly . . . subject Poins implies that Hal would be only too pleased if his father was sick.
obduracy Insensitivity.
persistency Persistence in loose pursuits.
Let the end try the man Let me be judged by how I turn out.
ostentation Outward appearance.
keeps the roadway i.e. is more conventional, orthodox.
accites Causes.
engraffed Closely bound up with.

on Of.
second brother A younger son, possessed of no inheritance.
proper . . . hands A good chap in a fight.
Christian i.e. a decent human being.
ape Presumably the page has been decked out in fantastic garb by his new master.
pottle-pot Tankard. One of many references to Bardolph's drinking habits (hence his fantastical red face and nose – the butt of much humour).
red lattice Windows of the taverns of the time were often made of red lattice. Bardolph's face is so red that the page could not tell window from man.
ale-wife Barmaid (presumably wearing red petticoats).
profited i.e. from his serving of Falstaff.
Althaea The page has it wrong: it was Althaea who dreamed that her son would live only so long as a log in the fire remained unburned.
A crown i.e. a reward for the page's 'wit'.
cankers Worms.
gallows . . . wrong The gallows will have been denied its due.
martlemas i.e. Falstaff. The Feast of St Martin (11 Nov) – the reference is probably to Falstaff being in the autumn of his life. Beef which had been fattened during the summer was slaughtered on this day.
immortal part Soul.
wen Lump.
place Rank.
borrower's cap Often removed from the head, to receive money.
Japhet One of Noah's sons – supposedly the father of Europeans (Genesis, 10, 5).
nearest i.e. eldest son.
certificate i.e. in the style of a formal document.
Romans Their brevity of style had become almost proverbial.
frank Sty.
Ephesians Paul rebuked the church at Ephesus for its immorality.
pagan Whore.
road Prostitute.
drawers Tapsters.
god . . . bull Refers to Jupiter's transformation, when he wished to woo Europa.
the purpose . . . folly The object in view must be weighed with the foolery involved (and in this case, excused therefore).

Act II Scene 3

Lady Northumberland seeks to persuade her husband not to join with the Archbishop against the King. Lady Percy, widow of Hotspur, adds her voice to the plea – it is obvious that she has in her mind the fact that Northumberland did not support her husband in his hour of need before Shrewsbury. Thus her pleadings take the form of a rebuke. Northumberland at first claims that his honour is at stake, but soon he gives in to his wife and daughter-in-law and determines to seek safety in Scotland.

Commentary

Shakespeare presents Northumberland in a very poor light. Once again, for motives of personal safety, he is seen to be letting down his friends. His departure for Scotland is cowardly. Pity is aroused for Lady Percy, who still grieves for her valiant husband, Hotspur. Her remarks hark back to the events of the earlier play and we are reminded therefore of the feat which Prince Henry performed when he killed Hotspur. We inevitably measure the Hal of the previous scene against the Prince who won his spurs in battle.

even . . . affairs Help smooth my way at these troublesome times.
Percy i.e. Northumberland himself.
pawn Stake.
stuck Stood out plainly.
vault of heaven i.e. the skies.
no legs . . . gait Anyone who had legs imitated his manner of walking.
thick Quickly (probably).
tardily Slowly, clearly.
turn . . . abuse Would mar their own perfections.
affections of delight That which gave pleasure.
humours of the blood Temperamental moodiness.
mark Aim.
defensible Capable of being defended.
ghost Spirit.
abide a field Take the field of battle.
precise Deeply involved.
nice Fastidious, over-careful.
Monmouth Prince Henry.
Beshrew A mild oath.
taste Trial.
ground Ascendancy.
suffer'd Permitted.
rain . . . heaven Lady Percy sees herself shedding tears like rain which will water, and cause to grow, the plant of memory.
recordation Remembrance.

Act II Scene 4

The Tavern in Eastcheap. Falstaff meets with the Hostess and Doll Tearsheet – for whom, it appears, he has some affection. Proceedings are interrupted by the arrival of the Ancient Pistol, whose rant and swagger so annoy the assembled company that Falstaff eventually expels him from the tavern. The Prince and Poins enter disguised as waiters and listen in wonder as Doll and Falstaff speak mutual endearments. Soon they overhear Falstaff speak disparagingly of themselves – at which point they declare themselves, and Falstaff vainly attempts to excuse himself for the abuse which he had previously heaped upon them. A knocking heralds the entrance of Peto with the message that the King has arrived at Westminster and that Falstaff has been asked for by 'a dozen sweating captains'. The Prince and Poins depart. A further message arrives to the effect that Falstaff's presence is required at court. He decides to leave, but not apparently before he has enjoyed the consolations of Doll Tearsheet.

Commentary

The 'apple-johns' to which the Drawers refer, inevitably remind us of Sir John, who is also 'old, round and withered'. It's a joke, of course, but the point is made – to be reinforced throughout much of this scene: Falstaff is no longer what he was – the grave beckons. The promise of 'old Utis' whets the audience's appetite: the expectation might be for a tavern scene to match the one in *Henry IV Part 1*, when Falstaff returned from his 'running away' at Gad's Hill.

The conversation between Doll and Falstaff is essentially good-humoured: we may suppose some genuine affection between prostitute and client. But one cannot help noticing that much of the talk is of disease, and we may catch a note of melancholy in Doll's remark: 'Come, I'll be friends with thee, Jack . . . there is nobody cares.'

Pistol is a wonderful comic creation: his speech is largely rant, derived from misquoted snatches from the dramatic tragedy which had enjoyed popularity in the theatre. This style was rapidly becoming dated. Pistol himself is also a familiar dramatic figure – the 'miles gloriosus' – a soldier of fortune who is bombastic and grandiose and entirely lacking in substance. Pistol is a mere 'tame cheater', despite all his threats and posturing – he is easily driven out, deflated, by Falstaff and Bardolph. This is the nearest that the scene comes to 'old Utis'.

Whilst Falstaff embraces and talks with his whore, the Prince and Poins, disguised as Drawers, overhear the conversation and comment on what they observe. The mood here is subtly contrived and may be appreciated on several levels: of course, most obviously it is comic – we watch Falstaff disparaging the Prince and Poins, and are aware that he will have to extricate himself from the trap into which he is falling. In essence, this is not dissimilar from the previous tavern scene in *Henry IV Part 1*. We may note, however, that the plot itself is not really comparable with the Gad's Hill episode. In the earlier play, the scheme was elaborately contrived and pursued with much vigour. There is not much life in this particular scheme, it does not seem to be executed with much enthusiasm and Falstaff's 'escape' (fizzling out in a mere reiteration of 'No abuse, Hal . . . ') is very feeble.

The comedy is not the main focus of interest: we must look elsewhere. It is significant that this is the last scene in which Hal and Falstaff are together, before the rejection of Falstaff in the final scene of the play (V 5). In a sense, Falstaff and Hal are not 'together' – in an amused/cynical manner, the Prince seems detached as he observes Falstaff and Doll. Indeed, the Prince's sardonic remarks are as powerful an influence upon the scene as the so-called 'comic' element. We are invited to see Falstaff and Doll through the Prince's eyes – but there is still more to see. Falstaff in *Henry IV Part 1* had always shown an awareness of the need for repentance – but his remarks on the subject had been flippant. Here, the references to growing old and the proximity of the grave have a deeper sense of reality. We are vividly aware of the knight's decay and grossness: he is ailing and diseased. The fact is that his whole life has been based upon illusion. Falstaff cannot 'escape' age, decay and death. Falstaff is not, nor ever has been, the Prince's mentor; he performed no heroic deeds at Shrewsbury; he is not young; he is not virtuous; he will never be 'sent for'. The image of an old man embracing his whore (a peddlar of dreams) is a powerful distillation of the illusions on which his life has been based.

Yet we must not forget, in the midst of these infirmities, that, despite ourselves, we have grown to love Falstaff. Despite his sinfulness, his sense of fun and the sheer effrontery of his wit has often endeared us mightily to him. As we see him in his decline, therefore, it is impossible not to recall what he was, and thus we can also feel the pathos of the situation. Possibly, at this point, we may see Falstaff as Everyman: like all humanity he would cheat the facts of age and death.

At the end of the scene 'reality' intervenes. In response to the demands of the world, the Prince departs. Falstaff is 'summoned' (in more senses than one, perhaps). After one last fling with Doll, he must to the wars.

apple-johns Apples which could be kept for a long time after they had been picked.
noise Musicians.
Dispatch Hurry up!
anon At once.
old utis A fine old time: 'utis'=muddle.
temperality A mixing of 'temper' and 'quality'.
pulsidge The pulses of the body.
canaries A sweet wine.
searching i.e. searches out every part of the body.
perfumes Pervades.
hem A belch.
When Arthur . . . king A snatch from a popular ballad.
jordan Chamber-pot.
calm Qualm.
muddy Out of season.
rascal Deer.
diseases i.e. venereal diseases.
joy My pet.
our chains and our jewels You take possession of the valuables which clients have given us.
ouches Brooches, and possibly V.D. scabs.
serve Falstaff here, and for the rest of the speech, puns obscenely: the military and the sexual phraseology form the basis of the joke.
conger Eel, or penis.
rheumatic The Hostess probably means choleric (hot-tempered).
confirmities Infirmities.
bear Put up with trouble; bear the weight of a man; bear children.
emptier vessel Another obscene remark.
hogshead Cask, also refers to the mighty girth of Falstaff.
Pistol A noisy unreliable weapon. Particularly apposite name for the good Ancient (ensign; standard-bearer).
civil Good-mannered.
cheater Card-sharp.
Barbary hen Whore.
charge you Drink your health.
discharge An obvious sexual innuendo.

bullets Testicles.
pistol-proof Proof against your advances; is past child-bearing.
cutpurse Pickpocket.
cuttle Cutpurse.
bottle ale All froth.
basket-hilt stale juggler Feeble swordsman. 'Basket-hilts' protected the hands.
points Laces for holding up the hose.
mouldy stewed prunes 'Stews' were brothels, hence 'disgusting old whores'.
occupy Another word for sexual intercourse.
Pluto's damnèd lake Presumably he means Lethe or Styx which were, in fact, rivers. Pluto=god of the Underworld.
Erebus The Underworld.
faitors Imposters.
Hiren Iron, or possibly a reference to a well-known play *Irene* by George Peele.
aggravate She means precisely the opposite.
hollow pampered jades of Asia A misquotation from Marlowe's *Tamburlaine*.
Troyant Trojan.
King Cerberus Cerberus was the three-headed dog which guarded the gates of the Underworld.
toys Trifles.
Calipolis The name of the heroine of another contemporary play. Pistol is much given to misquoting and speaking in the same style as the rant-tragedies of the times.
Si fortune . . . contento It sounds good but Pistol is not speaking any known language. The motto seems to mean: 'If fortune torments me, then hope contents me'.
points Stops.
etceteras Probably female genitalia.
neaf Hand.
the seven stars The Pleiades. He means that they have spent many a night together, out of doors.
fustian Bombastic.
Galloway nags Common horses that anyone may ride, hence 'whores'.
Quoit Pitch.
shove-groat An ancestor of 'shove ha'penny'.
incision Cutting (and the letting of blood, therefore).
imbrue Bloodshed.
abridge Cut short.
Untwind Untwine.
the Sisters Three The three Fates: Clothos, Atropos and Lachesis. The 'thread of life' was held on the spindle of Clothos, drawn to a certain length by Lachesis and finally cut by Atropos.
ape Fool.

Agamemnon Commanded the Greeks at the seige of Troy.
Nine Worthies Nine heroes, who set an example to all men: Hector, Julius Caesar, Alexander, Joshua, David, Judas Maccabeus, King Arthur, Charlemagne and the Crusader, Godfrey of Bouillon.
canvas Catch you, as if in a net.
like a church i.e. you will be as immovable as a church.
tidy Bonny.
Bartholomew boar-pig A pig was roasted to celebrate the Feast of Saint Bartholomew (24 August).
foining Thrusting.
pantler Pantryman.
chipped bread i.e. cut the crusts off bread.
Tewkesbury mustard Renowned for its sharp taste rather than its thickness. Falstaff's wit lets him down here and he unwittingly praises Poins in this misuse of simile.
conceit Imagination.
of a bigness i.e. of about the same size.
conger The flesh of the conger-eel was heavy and indigestible and was thought to render one stupid.
flap-dragons A silly pub-game where the participant sank his drink in which there floated some burning object e.g. a candle-end. The art was to quaff the drink without getting a burned mouth.
rides the wild mare Another childish game.
the sign of the Leg Bootmakers hung a boot outside their shops as a mark of their trade.
bate Contention.
gambol Playful.
nave The hub of a wheel. A reference to Falstaff's rotundity.
withered elder Both a withered elderly man and a withered elder-tree.
Saturn and Venus Heavenly bodies which symbolized Age and Love.
fiery Trigon The so-called 'trigon' were the three brightest signs in the heavens: Aries, Leo and Sagittarius. Refers to Bardolph's face.
tables Note-books.
busses Kisses.
kirtle Dress.
compound Lump.
take not the heat Continue the conversation.
candle-mine A reference to the fat which hangs from Falstaff – candles could be 'mined' from him.
close Be on our side.
dead elm Another reference to Falstaff's age and decrepitude.
pricked Marked down.
privy Personal, private.
malt-worms Drunkards.
burns poor souls A reference to Doll, from whom men catch V.D. – a symptom of which is a 'burning' sensation when passing water.
quit Pays back.

indictment Accusation.
flesh to be eaten i.e. running a bawdy-house.
joint of mutton A slang term for a prostitute.
posts Messengers.
profane Misuse.
commotion Civil war.
south i.e. the South Wind.
Borne . . . vapour Bearing black clouds.
post Post-haste.
peascod-time i.e. the time when peas are full in their pods (early summer).
blubbered With a face stained by tears.

Revision questions on Act II

1 Write an account of the character of Pistol.

2 How sympathetic (or otherwise) do you find Falstaff in this Act?

3 What are the aspects of the Prince's frame of mind that you find most significant in this Act?

4 How do you react to Falstaff's dealings with Doll Tearsheet?

5 What evidence have you found in the Act that Northumberland is an entirely unsympathetic character?

Act III Scene 1

In his palace at Westminster, King Henry IV, unable to sleep and ailing, feels himself weighed down by the troubled times, which seem to fulfil the prophecy of Richard II that Northumberland would turn against him. Warwick discounts the supernatural force of Richard's prophecy – seeing it as merely a shrewd political guess, based upon a knowledge of the character of Northumberland. Warwick believes that the country's ills are not beyond remedy: an army has already been dispatched sufficient to defeat Northumberland, and Owen Glendower (one of the rebel leaders) is dead. The King is somewhat mollified and utters a wish to embark upon a crusade, once the civil strife is over.

Commentary

The theme of sickness in the body politic is seen to be reflected in the King, who is disturbed and unable to sleep. Warwick's assurance that the kingdom's disease may be cured is an encouraging sign, but his optimism cannot apply to the King himself, who is part of the old order. Indeed, by his act of regicide in murdering Richard II, the King is mainly responsible for the sickness which haunts England. Shakespeare, through the utterance of the King, reminds us of the recent history which has led up to the events of this play. The arch-betrayer here is seen to be Northumberland. In passing, we may note that sleeplessness in Shakespeare is often a sign of guilt. The King's desire to launch a crusade is further evidence that he sees the expedition as a means of assuaging his guilt.

soft i.e. gentle, loving.
smoky cribs Smoke-filled hovels.
pallets Straw mattresses, beds.
dull god i.e. the god of sleep, who induces dullness (drowziness).
watch-case Sentry-box.
rude imperious surge The rough, all-conquering seas.
ruffian billows Boisterous waves.
top i.e. the topmost part of the waves.
deafing Deafening.
partial sleep i.e. favouring those who *can* sleep.
appliances Devices designed to induce slumber.
rank Swollen.
yet distemper'd Merely out of order.
the beachy . . . hips The girdle of the beach widens as the sea retreats.
check'd and rated Rebuked and berated.
head Gathering to a head (as a boil).
main chance The main drift of events.
come to life Come into being.
weak . . . intreasured In their early immature days lie treasured up for the future.
hatch Offspring, to be brooded over.
instance Proof.
unseasoned hours i.e. these latter times.
out of hand Over and done with.

Act III Scene 2

In deepest Gloucestershire the Justices Shallow and Silence (aptly named) await the arrival of Sir John Falstaff, who is enlisting soldiers for the forthcoming campaign. Like Sir John, both Justices are old men and Shallow constantly reminisces about his young days as a law student in London, when he kept company with the young Sir John Falstaff. Sir John arrives and he proceeds to enlist some of the pathetic creatures who are presented to him. Shallow launches into a series of recollections about his youth, including some boasts about his doings with certain 'bona-robas'. Falstaff recruits his soldiers dishonestly. In his final soliloquy, Falstaff expresses his contempt for Shallow, whose exploits were apparently not so awe-inspiring as he would have us believe. Nonetheless Falstaff intends to return later to squeeze some money from the gullible Shallow.

Commentary

As Shallow bustles about, eagerly awaiting the arrival of Falstaff, Shakespeare's comedy reveals the infirmities of old age and the simplicities of country life. The tone is sympathetic. Shallow, and his 'straight man' Silence, are essentially harmless and good-natured. We are invited to laugh at and feel for the propensity of old men to live in the past and to exaggerate the feats of their youth; we smile at the lapses of memory and the sudden non-sequitors – sometimes allied with a certain rustic shrewdness: 'How a good yoke of bullocks at Stamford Fair?'

The arrival of Falstaff heralds a darker tone to the comedy – his methods of recruiting are dishonest and designed to line his pocket: men are permitted to buy out their services and their places are taken by manifestly unsuitable candidates. Perceiving that there will be profit in it, Falstaff plays up to the nostalgic ramblings of Shallow – yet no sooner is he alone than he is pouring contempt upon him: Falstaff soon intends to 'fetch off these justices'. We are aware at this time of the clash between the ways of the country and the exploitative methods of the town.

rood Cross.
woosel Blackbird. It was not fashionable to be dark.
bona-robas High-class prostitutes.
Scoggin's The name means jester.
Stockfish Dry fish – hence an impotent man.
clapped . . . score Hit the bullseye at a range of 240 yards. Presumably a great feat of archery, perhaps exaggerated here.

forehand . . . half Technical archery terms – referring to sighting the arrow by using the bowhand as the foresight.
backsword man i.e. he practised with a wooden sword (with a basketwork hilt).
Accommodated Presumably a new word in Shakespeare's day.
in commission i.e. bearing the King's Commission as a Justice of the Peace.
sufficient Adequate.
roll List (of recruits).
singular Remarkably.
Prick . . . prick Put him down (enlist). Also carries a secondary sexual meaning.
old dame Old wife.
husbandry Household affairs.
spent Used up. Also a bawdy implication.
thy father's shadow . . . An elaborate pun involving 'sun' and 'son' and implying that he may be his father's son only upon shadowy evidence.
substance i.e. in reality the supposed father may not be the real father.
shadows . . . muster-book Alludes to the recruiting of non-existent men – for whom pay was drawn.
leader . . . thousands Presumably Wart is covered with thousands of warts or fleas.
gown Dressing-gown.
ring for thee i.e. the funeral bell, when he falls in battle.
Windmill Presumably a brothel.
ten shillings . . . crowns A considerable sum of money.
lief Rather.
quit i.e. is not indebted to.
thews Muscles.
assemblance Appearance.
charge . . . discharge Load and fire.
pewterer's hammer i.e. with rapidity, quick-fire.
come off . . . brewer's bucket Nimbly advances and retreats. Performs as quickly as a man fixes slings on a beer barrel when it is to be hoisted?
caliver Musket.
chopt Wizened.
scab Fellow, rascal.
tester Sixpence.
Sir Dagonet . . . show King Arthur's court jester. The 'show' was a display by a company of archers – each took the name of one of the Round Table knights.
quiver Nimble.
Bounce The sound of a musket, when fired.
fetch off Cheat, deceive.
prate Talk too much.
duer . . . tribute More duly than tribute paid to a Sultan by a vassal state.

Clement's Inn Another of the Inns of Court.
cheese-paring i.e. a man fashioned in cheese rind.
forlorn Meagre.
genius Spirit, essence of.
rearward of fashion Behind the times.
overscutched housewives Worn-out whores.
carmen Carters.
Vice's dagger Vice was a character in the Morality Plays of the pre-Elizabethan period. A figure of fun, he carried a wooden dagger.
tilt-yard i.e. where tournaments were held. Possibly Westminster.
burst . . . men Broke his head whilst jostling among the marshal's men (who controlled proceedings at tournaments). John of Gaunt = Henry IV's father.
treble hautboy The tiniest of the oboe family.
beefs Oxen.
philosopher's two stones The 'Philosopher's Stone' was required to enable alchemists to change base metal into gold. Falstaff implies that duping Shallow will be very profitable.
dace A small fish.

Revision questions on Act III

1 Give an account of the King's state of mind in the first scene of the Act.

2 How should we regard Falstaff's recruiting methods?

3 Discuss the presentation of Shallow and Silence.

4 How far do you find that the darker elements of Scene 2 overshadow the comedy?

Act IV Scene 1

At Gaultree, in Yorkshire, the rebel leaders meet with Westmoreland, emissary of John of Lancaster (general of the King's army). Northumberland's defection has left the rebels in a parlous condition, but they state their grievances with spirit, if no great precision. Westmoreland is openly contemptuous of the rebels, but he agrees to take their grievances and conditions of peace to Prince John. Mowbray is defiant, suspicious and not optimistic of peace. Hastings believes that terms can be agreed upon – and thus a fight may be avoided. The Archbishop inclines to Hastings. Westmoreland returns and the rebel leaders agree to meet Prince John at a point midway between the two armies.

Commentary

The weakness of the Archbishop's forces is at once apparent: Northumberland, true to his impotent, treacherous self has left them in the lurch. Shakespeare takes another opportunity to review the historical background which has preceded this moment in the play: in this instance we are reminded of the scene at the tournament in Coventry when Richard II banished Bolingbroke (now Henry IV) and Norfolk (Mowbray's father).

The rebels are shown to have no very precise reasons for their insurrection, but rather seem to be suffering from a general sense of grievance at Henry IV's slighting of them. Certainly we are given no good cause to side with them.

The stage is now set for Prince John's act of duplicity – which shows him to be a true son of his father: we can hardly side with him, either, in what is about to ensue. The next scene follows without a break.

Gaultree A forest which stretched to the north of York.
discoverers Scouts.
tenor Tone.
hold . . . quality As befits his rank.
ripe Bring to readiness.
overlive Outlive.
fearful meeting Dangerous clash.
opposite Opponent.
touch ground Reach rock bottom.
sway on Advance.
well-appointed Well-equipped.
fronts Confronts.
like itself i.e. in its true form.
abject routs Wretched mobs.
countenanc'd Approved by.
beggary Beggars.
damn'd commotion Cursed insurrection.
dress To deck out, give goodly outward shape to.
see The diocese of York.
Whose beard . . . i.e. the Archbishop has grown old whilst enjoying peace.
figure Symbolize.
translate Transform.
point of war i.e. the trumpet-call which signals battle.
surfeiting Over-indulgence.
wanton Wasteful.
bleed i.e. let blood (in battle), and be bled (as if by a surgeon).

take not on Do not take on the role of a physician.
show Demonstrate the true nature of.
diet rank . . . happiness Prescribe a healthy diet for sick minds.
griefs Grievances.
our most quiet there i.e. our times of perfect peace.
occasion The present situation.
articles Precise terms.
yet-appearing Still to be seen.
Concurring Brings together both name and fact.
galled Pained.
suborn'd Instigated.
grate Cause you annoyance.
brother general The Archbishop claims to be fighting for all men, whom he refers to here as his 'brothers'.
Construe Interpret.
to According to.
necessities i.e. that which we believe to be necessarily true.
signories Rightful possessions, lands.
breath'd i.e. given renewed life.
force perforce Whether he liked it or not.
seats Saddles.
daring . . . spur i.e. ready to spring into action.
beavers Visors (on their helmets).
warder Staff of office (at a tournament).
indictment Legal accusation.
miscarried Perished.
Hereford i.e. Bolingbroke (now Henry IV).
ne'r had borne it Would never have carried (the prize) from Coventry.
everything set off Everything set aside.
policy Scheming, deceit.
overween Think about it too carefully.
ken Sight.
battle Forces.
names Men of note.
reason will Reason dictates that.
rotten . . . handling i.e. your case is so rotten that it comes apart once it is 'handled', or given serious consideration.
commission Powers, granted by the King.
ample virtue Full authority.
general i.e. John of Lancaster.
muse I am surprised that.
several Individual.
ensinew'd to this action Firmly bound up in the cause.
substantial form Solid and formal (pardon).
aweful Worthy of awe.
banks i.e. they will come to flow again in their proper course.
diff'rence Conflict.

nice Insignificant.
wanton Trivial.
royal faiths . . . love If our loyalty to the King were tested even to the death.
partition Division.
dainty . . . picking Trivial . . . petty.
in the heirs of life i.e. those who inherit from those whom the King has 'ended'.
tables Notebooks.
precisely Scrupulously.
misdoubts Suspicions.
offensive Provoking.
resolv'd correction i.e. the chastisement which he has resolved upon.
offer We may make to attack.
atonement Agreement.
just distance Midway.

Act IV Scene 2

Prince John, after condemning the rebels, agrees to redress their grievances. Peace is offered and accepted. The order is given to disband the opposing armies. The rebel forces disperse but the King's forces do not follow suit. The rebel leaders are promptly arrested and sent to execution. John gives the order that the rebel forces should be rigorously pursued.

Commentary

Central to this scene, and to the political plot of the play, is the cold-blooded deception which Prince John practises upon his foes. His leading of them to believe that their wrongs shall be righted is cleverly done, and their weakness clearly does not put them in much of a position to resist him. Politics is shown to be a dirty business and John is thoroughly unlikable. Particularly abhorrent is the manner in which he disguises his chicanery by a mere form of words (he will redress the grievances, but he does not say that he would pardon the grieved). No chivalry here: his actions compare badly with Hal's defeat of Hotspur at Shrewsbury. *Henry IV Part 2* is altogether a 'darker' play than *Part 1*. Cynicism is further heightened by John's attributing the 'victory' to God and his promise to exercise 'Christian care', as well as mentioning that 'honour' demands that he redress the rebels' grievances. Such ironies would not be lost on Shakespeare's audience. Ironically, too, he condemns the Archbishop's godly facade, early on in the scene. This should not lead us to sympathize unduly with the rebels: their motives have always been presented as essentially selfish – in this scene like meets like.

iron In armour.
Cheering Encouraging.
word to sword The word of God is being used to give a dignity to the use of force.
Would If he intends to.
abroach Reveal.
books of God i.e. spiritual matters.
speaker As in the modern House of Commons.
opener Revealer.
intelligencer Interpreter.
dull workings The paltry workings of our minds.
countenance Face, appearance.
ta'en up Recruited.
counterfeited Pretended.
zeal Enthusiasm.
his substitute The King was believed to be God's earthly deputy.
up-swarm'd Gathered them together in a swarm.
common sense As may be obvious to anybody.
monstrous Hideous, against nature.
hold . . . up Maintain our safety.
Hydra According to Classical mythology the Hydra was a many-headed, deadly snake. No sooner was one head lopped off, than another grew in its place.
of this madness i.e. once the King has granted us a cure for this insanity of rebellion (by redressing our grievances).
tamely to the foot i.e. pay homage, kneel in obedience.
second Support.
theirs i.e. more reinforcements.
success Succession of.
generation i.e. the power to beget children.
sound Test the depths of.
after-times The future.
lavishly Freely.
Wrested Twisted.
their i.e. the eyes of the assembled armies.
breed Nurture.
happy season At a very appropriate moment. Mowbray despises the current proceedings.
Against In expectation of.
heaviness Sadness.
passing Exceptionally.
if your own rule be true i.e. if your earliest precept holds good.

trains Followers.
cop'd withal Fought with.
charge Command.
sporting-place Place of recreation.
attach Arrest.
pawn'd Pledged.
Meet Fitting for.
stray Soldiers, who have just been disbanded.

Act IV Scene 3

On the strength of his reputation, Falstaff persuades Colevile of the Dale to surrender to him, and he duly presents his captive to Prince John. The Prince is unimpressed with Falstaff's boasting. The pursuit of the rebels is halted; Colevile is sent to his death. Falstaff is permitted to leave for Gloucestershire and he eagerly anticipates the gulling of Shallow. Before he departs, however, Falstaff extols the virtues of sherris-sack.

Commentary

Falstaff's capture of Colevile is a pale echo of his monstrous claiming of Hotspur's scalp after the battle at Shrewsbury. John's shabby treatment of Colevile further underlines the tawdriness of the whole episode at Gaultree. Again the absence of chivalry is noteworthy; in its place we find cold, inglorious efficiency.

If the scene has any glory, it is to be found in Falstaff's eulogy of 'good sherris-sack'. Intellect tells us that what he says is nonsense; yet it makes a kind of sense, and unlike much of what Falstaff has to say in this play, it is genuinely witty. The reality is that sack induces drunkenness and lack of order in the body: typically, Falstaff is able to make disorder sound attractive, as his enthusiasm blinds us to the true effects of the drink. The lip-smacking way in which Falstaff anticipates the gulling of Shallow is not very edifying.

condition Rank.
drops of thy lovers Falstaff implies that if he is made to sweat in taking Colevile, then those who love him will be forced to shed tears! (i.e. for Colevile's death).
school Multitude.
indifferency i.e. not of any particular note.

womb Belly.
tardy tricks Habit of shirking.
check Reproof.
motion Powers of movement.
expedition of thought The speed of thought.
extremest . . . possibility As fast as I possibly could.
foundered Caused to break down.
posts Post-horses. Horses which were used in relays.
courtesy Good-breeding.
particular ballad Special ballad. Heroic deeds were often celebrated in ballads – with the hero's picture inscribed above the printed version.
gilt twopences i.e. fake coins. Silver twopences were sometimes gilded so that they could be passed off as gold coins.
cinders of the element i.e. the stars, which shine feebly in comparison with the moon.
won Gained victory over.
deaer At greater cost to yourself.
stay'd Halted.
present Immediate.
dispatch Hasten.
Stand Take my part as my patron.
proof Test.
fishmeals i.e. lacking in redbloodedness.
green-sickness A form of anaemia, common in young girls.
inflammation The stirring qualities induced by liquor.
sherris-sack A white wine from Xeres, in Spain much-beloved by Falstaff.
crudy Curdy, thick.
apprehensive Perceptive.
quick Lively.
forgetive Creative.
shapes Forms, images.
delivered o'er Passed on to.
wit Intelligence.
settled Lifeless.
liver Believed to be the seat of the passions.
extremes i.e. the extremities.
little kingdom The notion that the human body was analogous to the body politic was commonplace in Shakespeare's day.
petty spirits The human body, it was believed, was given life by the action of certain vital spirits (or fluids).
commences it Gives it (academic!) status. Awards it a degree.
Hereof From this.
lean Poor, infertile.
manured Farmed.
husbanded Cultivated.

potations Drinks.
tempering Softening (normally applied to wax).
seal Seals were made of wax.

Act IV Scene 4

The dying King instructs his youngest son, Clarence, that he should support Hal when he becomes Henry V. Hal's absence is noted and Clarence informs his father that the heir-apparent is still consorting with his Eastcheap cronies. The King's confidence in Hal evaporates, and he forthwith launches into a lament on the ill-fortune which he believes will await England when Hal becomes King. Warwick defends the Prince. They are interrupted by news of the rebels' defeat – but the King can take no pleasure in the tidings: in pain, he is borne away.

Commentary

The King's optimism gives way to despair: this may be surprising because he must surely by now be aware of the true merit of his son – yet he seems all too willing to assume that Hal has slipped back into his wicked ways. We must remember, however, that he is clearly a dying man and therefore his judgement is clouded. Warwick provides a counterbalancing opinion of Hal: his speech reminds us of the intentions which Hal expressed throughout *Henry IV Part 1*.

Clarence, who had ironically been asked to play a harmonizing role *vis-à-vis* Hal, brings dissension with his betrayal of Hal's whereabouts. Also, it is apparent that the King has quickly forgotten his own expressed estimate of his son.

There is a feeling in this scene of the passing of the old order. We are reminded of the dubious manner of Henry IV's accession, but the final defeat of the rebels seems to close that particular chapter (for the time being, at least). There is also the reminder that Hal may, with some justification, claim the kingship by right of succession. We should not be blinded, however, to the fact that the basis of even Hal's kingship is blighted by the usurpation of his father: the reign of Henry V provides only a temporary respite – the house of Lancaster is doomed. (See Shakespeare's *Henry VI* tetralogy).

debate Conflict.
higher fields Nobler fields of battle (a Crusade).
address'd Prepared.
power Army.
substitutes i.e. those who will deputize for the King.
invested Given authority.
level In accord with.
effect Perform.
omit Neglect.
grace Royal favour.
observ'd Given proper attention.
humourous Moody.
sudden Unpredictable.
flaws . . . of day Snowflakes at daybreak.
scope Make allowances.
on ground i.e. beached.
Confound Defeat.
working Exertion, the struggle.
hoop of gold A metaphor suggesting that Clarence will be able to bind his brothers together, just as a hoop binds together a cask ('vessel').
suggestion Suspicion.
force perforce Whether you like it or not.
aconitum Wolf's bane. A poison.
rash Violent.
fattest Most fertile.
shape Imagine.
unguided days Anarchy.
rage Passion.
means i.e. the means to put his will into practice.
lavish manners Unrestrained behaviour.
affections Desires.
oppos'd Hostile.
beyond him i.e. you do not see him as he really is.
immodest Indecent.
mete Measure.
carrion Rotting flesh.
course Event.
haunch Hinderpart.
shrieve Sheriff.
stomach Appetite.
hold out Sustain.
wrought the mure Constructed the wall.
Unfather'd i.e. virgin births.
loathly Loathsome, unnatural.
time's doting chronicles Foolish chronicles of supernatural events.
Edward Edward III.
sick'd Sickened.

Act IV Scene 5

Prince Hal watches by his sleeping father's bedside; he catches sight of the crown, which lies on a pillow. He picks it up and wanders from the chamber. The King awakes and mistakenly believes that Hal, unable to wait any longer for his death, has prematurely seized the great symbol of monarchy. Henry IV expresses his disgust at what he regards as Hal's indecent haste to be rid of him; he foresees a time of riot and dishonour, when Hal becomes king. Hal returns and sorrowfully, but with great dignity, reassures his father that he merely borrowed the crown 'to try with it as an enemy'. The King's fears are stilled and he goes on to offer Hal some shrewd advice: 'to busy giddy minds with foreign quarrels'. Sensing his imminent death, the King asks to be carried to the Jerusalem chamber – he perceives now the ironic truth of the prophecy that he should die in 'Jerusalem'.

Commentary

There is no pause between this scene and the previous one. Hal's speech addressed to the crown ('O polished perturbation! Golden care!) bears a striking resemblance to his father's earlier speech: 'Uneasy lies the head that wears a crown'. It is clear from what Hal says that he approaches his impending kingship with a feeling of high-seriousness and no little trepidation. Also apparent is the true affection in which he holds his father and the determination with which he intends to maintain that which has been so dearly won. It is tempting to see in the placing of the crown on his head a sort of 'mock-usurpation'. At any rate, this is how the king views it when he wakes up: a moment of agony ensues – the King's final punishment for his sins, before he comes to understand the true worth of the son he has fathered.

When King and Prince are alone together, we sense their closeness. After listening to his father's condemnation, Hal, in measured tones, is able to pacify the former's doubts and to reassure him that as king, he intends to maintain his grip on the throne. On a personal level, Henry IV is, for the moment, still king – and Hal will honour him as such until his death: there is to be no premature snatching of the crown; the King will not find himself 'usurped' by his own son. In this, Hal shows himself particularly sensitive to his father's lifelong fear of being deposed. Next, Hal quiets the other great fear of Henry IV: that his kingdom will become a place of riot and disorder. There is an irony here: throughout his reign Henry IV had sought to be a good king and to rule England well, but his usurpation of the rightful monarch (Richard II) had made this impossible – in murdering God's anointed king, he had called down upon himself and his kingdom a curse, which manifested itself in continual personal and political unrest. Now we find that Hal, about whose prospective reign many misgivings have been expressed, is about to bring the country a period of firm government, unity of purpose and military glory.

It cannot surprise us, in the light of the attitudes expressed in this scene, that Falstaff is to be rejected. There has been a literal distance between Hal and Falstaff throughout the play (they have appeared together only once). This moment in the play reveals the immense spiritual gulf which separates them. Again, it is perhaps ironic that there have been moments in this scene and the previous one, in which Henry IV and Falstaff have shared the same misconceptions about Hal and the kingdom which he will rule.

dull Soothing.
favourable Willing to undertake the favour for me.
changes Complexion changes.
heaviness Sadness.
Rain Refers to tears.
Perturbation Restlessness.
ports of slumber The eyes (ports=doors).
homely biggen Humble nightcap.
scald'st with safety i.e. whilst conferring safety on the wearer, nonetheless causes him to burn with the heat.
suspire Breathe.
rigol Circle.
Derives Passes down.
lineal Hereditary.
chide i.e. send him here with a rebuke.
part Action.
conjoins Is joined with.
nature i.e. human nature, natural feelings of affection.
engrossed Stored up.
strange-achieved Strangely won (perhaps by wicked means).
thoughtful Careful.
arts and martial exercises A gentleman was presumed to be master of the arts of both peace and war.

Yields . . . ending father i.e. thus the treasures which have been hard won by the father yield him a bitter taste at his death.
determin'd Ended.
kindly Natural.
deeper demeanour Serious bearing.
latest Last.
opinion i.e. general opinion.
soil dirt.
boisterous Rough, violent.
supposed i.e. peace which did not actually exist.
scene . . . argument i.e. as if he was participating in a play upon that topic.
purchas'd Rather than inherited.
garland i.e. the Crown.
successively According to the laws of inheritance.
fell Dread.
state Throne of state.
giddy Unstable, restless.
hence . . . out Carried out abroad.
waste Destroy.
pain Endeavour.
period Conclusion.
quaff'd Drank.
invest Endow.
cloud of dignity The figure suggests that the wind prevents the cloud from letting the rain fall ('wind' = the King's breath).
seal'd up Made final (in a legal sense).
whetted Sharpened.
forbear me Delay your onslaught upon me.
balm Holy oil (used to anoint a king).
compound Mix.
mock at form Scorn decency.
neighbour confines Neighbouring regions.
curb'd licence Restrained licentiousness.
flesh Satiate.
care What you really care about.
affect Earnestly desire, favour.
obedience Posture of obedience.
depending Dependent upon you (the crown).
med'cine potable Liquid gold was used in a medicine. Also a possible reference to the alchemists' 'elixir of life' (supposedly derived from gold) which was intended to confer immortality upon those who partook of it.
bearer Wearer.
strain Impulse, feeling of. (A term derived from music).
rebel Rebellious.
might Power (which it might confer).

Revision questions on Act IV

1 What are the grievances which Westmoreland hears from the Archbishop?

2 Describe how Prince John deceives the rebels.

3 What is your opinion of Prince John's trickery?

4 How far is Falstaff successful in his attempt to ingratiate himself with Prince John?

5 Has the King any justification for mistrusting Prince Hal?

6 How convincing do you find the Prince's explanation for his taking of the crown?

7 What light is thrown upon the King by his review of his own reign and his advice to the Prince for his reign?

Act V Scene 1

Justice Shallow now has Sir John with him in Gloucestershire once more. Davy (Shallow's servingman) is urged to make appropriate preparations and he does not lose the opportunity to support the case of one of his villainous friends before his master. Shallow agrees to show Davy's friend some partiality. Falstaff, who has yet to begin exploiting Shallow, notes the similarities between the justice and his servant – the stories he proposes to tell Hal about his visit to Gloucestershire, will, he is sure, be well-received and provide much mirth.

Commentary

The petty corruptions of the country justice mirror in comic form some of the mightier deceits and dishonesties which we have observed in the play. Here the mood is almost entirely comic: again much is made of Shallow's dithering agedness – easy meat for the shrewd Davy. The brooding presence of Falstaff (a mighty pike to Shallow's minnow) notes the conversation between Shallow and Davy in silence.

In a minor way, the expectation of Davy that he will carry some influence with Shallow brings to our notice a similar expectation in the mind of Falstaff: he, too, hopes for preferment when Prince Hal becomes king. In his turn, Shallow himself curries favour with Sir John in the hope that he may gain some influence at court – 'A friend i' the court is better than a penny in purse.'

William cook i.e. William the cook.
precepts Summonses.
hade land The land separating two ploughed areas.
note Account, bill.
plough-irons Ploughshares.
cast Added up.
link Chain (for lowering a bucket).
Hinckley A town near Stratford.
answer it Make good the deficit.
kickshaws Trifles.
backbitten i.e. by fleas.
conceited Conceived.
countenance Show favour to.
bear out Support.
quantities Portions, small lengths.
staves Walking-staffs, popularly carved with the head of a 'hermit'.
the semblable . . . his How closely servants resemble their masters.
their spirits i.e. how closely the character of the servant comes to resemble the justice.
in consent In common accord.
curry Curry favour with.
their company i.e. those with whom they keep company.
terms Court sessions.
actions Lawsuits.
intervallums Court 'recesses' (when the court is not in session).
sad brow Serious countenance.
ache Rheumatism.
laid up Stored away.

Act V Scene 2

The old King is dead. Anxiously the Lord Chief Justice and Warwick await the arrival of Henry V. They are soon joined by the King's brothers: Lancaster, Clarence and Gloucester. They all expect that the King will be eager to settle old scores; the mood is solemn. It is expected that Falstaff will be elevated to a secure position under the new régime.

With the arrival of the King, we become aware that things do follow the expected course. The King is gracious to his brothers: in return for their love and loyalty, he offers to become their 'father'. Henry now turns to the Chief Justice, who fully anticipates that he will be the recipient of the King's displeasure – after all, at one point in Hal's wild days he committed the heir apparent to prison. Henry reminds him of this action. Stoutly, the Chief Justice defends himself, whilst assuring the new King of his loyalty. Henry's response is to reaffirm the Chief Justice's office, to exonerate him for his former actions and to express the hope that he will continue to uphold the laws of the land. Finally, the King looks forward to ruling over an England which will 'rank with the best-governed nation'.

Commentary

In a play in which expectations are frequently confounded, we see this process vividly at work here. Hal does not live down to the expectations which others hold of him. His bearing on entry is formal and dignified; his affirmation that he will uphold the law takes the Chief Justice by surprise. It must be remarked also that Henry does not altogether cut an edifying figure in the scene: his 'playing' with the obvious trepidation of the Chief Justice seems unnecessary – designed to make a point, rather than spare the feelings of a man. There has always been this element of the player in Henry: throughout *Henry IV Part 1*, his actions were essentially a façade, his wildness no more than a scheme designed to gain the maximum impact from his reformation. This reformation is now upon us. Unfortunately, in discarding his wicked ways, it could be argued that Henry has become something of a prig. His moralizing cannot be faulted: it is what we expect from a king, perhaps – all the right sentiments are present. But still we lament the absence of warmth and we are left with a series of worthy, rather formal sentiments. All is clearly leading up to the rejection of Falstaff, whose days are numbered.

Exceeding well A euphemistic way of saying that he is dead.
the heavy issue His sorrowing children.
temper Temperament.
strike sail Lower their sails i.e. humble themselves.
argument The subject (of which they are talking).
fair i.e. speak well of him.
stream of quality The natural inclinations for a man of your qualities.
ragged . . . remission Beggarly and impossible pardon.
Amurath A sixteenth century Turkish Sultan who had all his brothers killed upon succeeding to the throne.

sad Serious.
appears i.e. in their appearance (mourning clothes).
deeply With all seriousness.
Harry lives He refers to himself, of course.
rate Chide.
easy Of no significance.
Lethe The river of forgetfulness in the Underworld – one sip was supposed to induce oblivion.
person i.e. I represented your father.
bench i.e. bench of justice.
mock your workings Show contempt towards your deeds.
second body i.e. as your representative.
propose Imagine yourself to be.
cold considerance Calm consideration.
state Character (as a king).
the balance and the sword The emblems of authority.
proper Own.
unstained Untarnished, uncorrupted.
remembrance Legal reminder.
intents Intentions.
well-practis'd Experienced.
gone wild He means that his wild deeds practised upon his father have followed his father into the grave.
affections Appetites.
spirits i.e. His father's spirit survives in him.
sadly In a serious frame of mind.
After . . . seeming According to the way that I have seemed to behave.
state of floods The majestic ocean.
In equal rank England may now be ranked with the best governed nations upon earth.
accite Summon.
remember'd Recorded.
state Statesmen.
consigning Ratifying, setting seal to.

Act V Scene 3

In Shallow's Gloucestershire a drunken gathering is in progress. Suddenly, Pistol bursts on the scene with the 'joyful' tidings that the King is dead. Falstaff welcome the news and believes that his time has come at last. Without delay, he proposes to set forth for the coronation of Henry V. He departs with his absurd retinue, promising them all favours under the new dispensation.

Commentary

Shakespeare has much fun at the expense of the tipsy Shallow and Silence. In the midst of things, to great comic effect on stage, the hitherto silent Silence bursts forth into song. The disorder of the scene is further heightened by the entrance of the ranting Pistol: in comic miniature we get another glimpse of the disordered society which would have been England, had Falstaff and his ilk gained pre-eminence. Of course, the irony of Falstaff's joyous reception of the news of Henry IV's death is abundantly apparent to an audience that anticipates the real reception which Falstaff is to receive when he arrives in London. In passing, it is worth noting that Silence's song, which refers to festivities before Lent, presages the 'Lenten' time which in fact awaits Falstaff and his followers.

graffing Grafting.
husband Steward.
varlet Servant.
Proface Welcome.
bear Bear with me.
Shrove-tide Festivities held just before Lent, ending with Shrove Tuesday. A time for confessions.
leather-coats A type of apple.
leman Sweetheart.
pledge . . . mile Drink your health from a cup a mile deep.
beshrew Cursed be.
cabileros Gallants.
pottle-pot A tankard containing two quarts.
out Drop out.
done me right Answered my drinking toast.
dub me knight A drinking term, expressing admiration for a feat.
Samingo A corrupt form of 'San Domingo', the hero of a drinking song.
Puff Presumably the name of a local man who was almost as fat as Falstaff.
recreant Cowardly.
helter-skelter With utmost speed.
this world Implies that Pistol has passed into the stratosphere!
foutre A contemptuous obscenity.
Africa Supposedly the place from which gold originated.
Assyrian With the emphasis on the 'ass'.
Cophetua Another figure from a contemporary ballad. An African.
Robin Hood, etc. More ballad heroes.
Helicons A mistake by Pistol. 'Helicon' was the name given to a range

of mountains in Greece – the home of Apollo and the Muses. Here it may be synonymous with 'poets'.
Furies Avenging goddesses of Greek mythology.
Besonian You ignorant bumpkin.
office Official status.
do this Presumably indicating an obscene gesture.
fig The 'fig' was a name given to a specific obscene gesture.
double-charge 'Charge' you twice over.
Boot Advantage, profit.
Where . . . led Snatch from an old ballad.

Act V Scene 4

Amid mighty protests and some physical violence, the Hostess and Doll are arrested by the beadle and his officers. They are to be whipped. There is a suspicion that they have been involved in the death of a man in the tavern.

Commentary

This is a brief but bitter scene. There has been a death at the Tavern. The violence against the women is nasty and brutish. Shakespeare clearly does not wish his audience to leave the theatre with a sense of triumph, amusement or exaltation. The mood is dark and threatening.

The short scenes at this point in the play have the effect of hastening us towards the final climatic scene: for Falstaff and his friends things are going downhill fast. Here we get a foretaste of what awaits Falstaff as he arrives in London.

Beadle An officer of the law, who punished petty offenders.
whipping-cheer The 'good cheer' of a flogging.
about In her presence.
Nut-hook A contemptuous reference to the beadle's staff.
tripe-visaged Pock-marked.
paper-faced White-faced.
cushions Implies that Doll is faking her pregnancy by stuffing cushions under her dress.
thin man in a censer A censer was used to fumigate rooms. Possibly the thin man refers to an image which was stamped on to a censer.
swinged Whipped.
blue-bottle Alludes to the blue coat worn by the beadle.
half-kirtles Skirts.
knight-errant Refers to the belligerent disposition of Doll.

right . . . might The Hostess, characteristically, is somewhat confused: she means precisely the opposite.
of sufferance From suffering.
atomy She means anatomy ('skeleton').
rascal Lean deer. Yet another allusion to the thin beadle.

Act V Scene 5

Falstaff and his followers have assembled in London, hoping to catch the King's eye as he processes through the streets on his coronation day. Falstaff anticipates the favours which he expects to be shown. As the King passes by Falstaff hails him – Henry does not respond but affects not to recognize him. Eventually, after addressing Falstaff as if he were a dimly remembered figure, the King rebukes the fat knight for his dissolute way of life and then banishes him from the royal presence. Unconvincingly, Falstaff attempts to laugh off the King's rejection of him – but no one seriously believes him when he says that he will be 'sent for'. The Lord Chief Justice enters only to send Falstaff and his company to prison. The Chief Justice and John of Lancaster express their satisfaction at the way things have turned out and look forward to a military expedition to France. The King has evidently heeded his father's advice.

Commentary

This scene juxtaposes two 'retinues': there is the King, surrounded by his glorious company, dressed in full coronation garb; and there is a travel-stained Falstaff surrounded by his motley crew. Shakespeare has left us in no doubt as to the outcome. Thus, as Falstaff speculates upon his advancement and makes promises that he cannot keep, it is impossible not to feel some pity for the old rogue. Much has been written about the speech in which the King rejects his erstwhile companion. Some critics find it priggish and almost entirely unsympathetic, and they damn the King accordingly. We might reply to this charge by reminding ourselves that, whatever the King may feel as a man, he cannot forget that he is now a King. This is a public disavowal of his former way of life and the rumours which have grown up around him. Any show of affection now might be interpreted as weakness. Furthermore, in the latter part of the speech, Henry does acknowledge Falstaff's needs when he grants him a small allowance. The administration of justice is left to the Lord Chief Justice, and Falstaff is taken off to prison. By distancing this moment from the person of the King himself, Shakespeare avoids too much odium attaching itself to Henry. Nonetheless, the irony of Falstaff's certainty that he will be 'sent for' is immediately apparent.

It is noteworthy that the final words of the play are given to Prince John. The ending is decidedly 'downbeat'. We cannot like Prince John, his conduct as Gaultree still rankles – here he looks forward with evident satisfaction to the onset of a new régime. His tone is gloating and smug – clearly he feels that his time has come, too.

rushes Normally used as a carpet.
grace Favour.
liveries Servants' uniform.
bestowed Spent at my tailors.
to shift me To change my clothes.
semper idem (Lat.) always the same.
obsque . . . est (Lat.) apart from this there is nothing.
all . . . part The whole of it.
liver Seat of the passions, notably love.
Helen i.e. the beauteous Helen of Troy.
durance Prison, confinement.
mechanical Workman's.
ebon Black.
fell Dread.
Alecto One of the avenging Furies of classical mythology. Her hair was wreathed in snakes.
imp Graft. Hal is seen to be one of the graftings of Fame personified.
Jove Chief of the Gods.
surfeit-swell'd Bloated with excesses.
profane Foul-mouthed.
hence In future.
gormandizing Gluttony.
fool-born Born of foolishness, prompted by folly.
competence of life In order that you may be sustained.
colour 1) a show 2) anger, 'choler' 3) a hangman's nose, 'collar' 4) the flag 'colours' of an enemy.
Fleet A prison in Fleet Street.
Si fortuna . . . contenta 'If fortune torments me, hope contents me'.
intent The intention that.
wonted Habitual.
civil swords i.e. those swords drawn in civil war.

The Epilogue

The Epilogue closes the play. We find the traditional mock-modesty and an appeal to the audience to view the play favourably. There is a looking forward to *Henry V* and an assurance that any resemblance between Falstaff and Sir John Oldcastle is purely coincidental.

Commentary

We may feel that an appeal to the audience to view the play sympathetically has a special force when we remember that they have just witnessed the discountenancing of Falstaff. The assurance that Falstaff was to appear in the next play (*Henry V*) may have mollified the audience, but it was promise that Shakespeare did not keep.

The assurance that Sir John Falstaff is not Sir John Oldcastle was probably included in deference to the Oldcastle family.

fear i.e. that the play will not have been well-received.
curtsy Bow.
undo Destroy.
venture The business.
a displeasing play Presumably refers to some unpopular contemporary drama.
unluckily home i.e. it returns to me again ill-received.
break Break my word, go 'broke' (financially).
Bate . . . some Excuse me from some of my debt to you.
use my legs To take him off-stage.
dance The Epilogue was spoken by a dancer.
light Insufficient.
Oldcastle According to some histories, Hal's companion was Sir John Oldcastle – in fact an honoured Protestant martyr. Shakespeare probably chose not to use his name in later versions of the play for fear of upsetting Oldcastle's family.

Revision questions on Act V

1 How do you regard Henry's dealing with the Lord Chief Justice in Scene 1?

2 Show how the play builds to the climatic final scene. In what ways is the rejection of Falstaff anticipated in the Act?

3 Do you find that the scenes in Gloucestershire in this Act differ in tone from the Gloucestershire scene in Act III? If you do, can you provide reasons for this difference?

4 Analyse carefully the speech in which Henry rejects Falstaff. Do you think Falstaff deserved his pension?

5 Do you find any pathos in the final scene of the play?

6 Why do you think that Shakespeare failed to keep his promise to present Falstaff in *Henry V*?

Shakespeare's art in *Henry IV Part 2*
Themes

Background to the historical theme

To orthodox medieval philosophers, the universe and everything in it was an ordered structure, created and presided over by God. Each constituent part of this 'cosmos' had a fixed rank, or value, and fulfilled a function according to the dictates of Divine Providence. The structure was hierarchical: at the top of the pyramid was the Creator, beneath came Angels, next Man, and so on down the scale until one reached the humblest forms of inanimate matter. Each broad category in the hierarchy was thought to be sub-divided into other hierarchies, and the whole was dependent upon its parts.

In the beginning all Creation was harmonious: God reigned in heaven. Man, in his rank below the Angels, was Lord of the Earth. The whole proclaimed the glory of the Creator. Unfortunately, through the misuse of free-will, Man sought to indulge his own appetites and place himself above the Law of God – he sought to become a god himself. The harmony between Man and God was broken: discord entered the world, as the result of sin. Man, or a man, might regain his favoured position in the Divine Scheme by virtue of God's Grace, but he had to be constantly on his guard lest he fall again into sin, by giving way to the appetites of his 'lower' or bestial self. The consequences of such a falling-off were manifestly horrendous, and affected not only the individual sinner but also had ramifications in the world around him. The more eminent the sinner, the more profound the sin, so the consequences were the more dire.

The King occupied the chief position in the hierarchy of the nation. He ruled by Divine Right – he was God's bailiff on earth. His right to be King was upheld by the hereditary principle. To overthrow and kill the rightful king was thus conceived as an act of sacrilege and invited the direst punishment from the Almighty. The usurper, inevitably, would come to experience Divine wrath and eventually His justice would be upheld. The nation could expect no peace until the will of God was re-established. In extreme circumstances, the very fabric of the heavens might become disordered: strange eclipses, tempests, comets were often supposed to be manifestations of Divine displeasure.

Tudor historians, adopting the orthodox standpoint, believed that history demonstrated the workings of God's justice and His vengeance. The period from the reign of Richard II to the death of Richard III was thought to reveal the workings of Divine Providence. Richard II, a 'bad' king, was nevertheless God's anointed ruler. Henry Bolingbroke, in deposing him, committed sacrilege, and, as a consequence, was 'punished' by civil unrest and a sense of personal guilt. There was a brief moment of respite under Henry V, who at least had some claim under the hereditary principle, but the whole country was plunged into the Wars of the Roses during the reign of Henry VI. The wicked Richard III, himself a regicide, purged the nation of the guilt of Bolingbroke's crime, before perishing himself at Bosworth. Finally, God's providence was reasserted by the accession of Henry Tudor, a rightful successor – and greatness was restored to the kingdom. By this means, a neat, schematic and propagandist interpretation was given to the chaos and bloodletting subsequent upon the usurpation of Richard II. In Shakespeare's time, the problem of who was to succeed the childless Elizabeth I loomed large: the last thing the nation wanted was a bloody struggle for the throne, contingent upon her death. The memory of the Wars of the Roses was an ever-present warning of what might happen.

Disorder

Disorder abounds in *Henry IV Part 1*. England is threatened by a rebellion, and not for the first time Henry IV finds himself forced to live out the consequences of his wresting of the crown from its true possessor. To put it another way, Henry, once an arch-rebel himself, now has to contend with rebellion: it may be allowed that Henry's rebellion was not motivated by self-interest – even his most cynical detractor would probably grant him a modicum of concern for the country's welfare. Nonetheless, he must live with the disorder wrought in his personality by the knowledge that he is a great sinner. Symptomatically, he cannot sleep, and by the time we meet him he is ravaged by disease: almost literally, worn out by the struggle to maintain his grip on the nation and himself – 'Uneasy lies the head that wears a crown'. To make matters worse, for much of the play the future looks bleak: his disorderly son keeps low company and cannot be relied upon not to render up his hard-won gains to the likes of Falstaff.

Falstaff, himself, is the personification of lawlessness: he is governed by appetite – his own will is his only law. Falstaff is a gormandizer, a womanizer, a liar. He does not pay debts; he misuses the King's Press; he is cowardly and only pretends to be brave; he fondly believes that when Hal is king, the laws will be 'at his commandment'.

Even the English countryside seems under the sway of the bumbling, vain and incompetent Shallow, who is prepared to bend the law to accommodate the wishes of a steward. In Gloucestershire we find that it is the courageous Feeble who is mocked for having aspirations other than those of pure self-interest.

The prevalence of disorder in the play is further increased by the presence of disease. Northumberland is sickly, Falstaff complains of the gout and there are many indications that he is paying the price for a lifetime's self-indulgence. The King, as we have seen, is a dying man. Shallow shows the signs of incipient senility. These and other references, notably in connection with Doll Tearsheet, contribute to the feeling that England is stricken: physical ailments mirror the infection in the body politic.

Shakespeare, by introducing his play with the 'character' Rumour, signposts the time which the play unfolds:

Rumour is a pipe
Blown by surmises, jealousies, conjectures. . .

Order

Against the disruptive forces which are ranged against them, the forces of order are ultimately triumphant. The rebellion is defeated and Hal is firmly established as Henry V – a king who is clearly going to keep a firm hand on the tiller of state. To aid him in his task, he has the Lord Chief Justice, a figure who is unflinchingly dedicated to the principle of law and order. Henry V's decision to launch a war against France is politically shrewd, for it will have the effect of uniting the country against a common foe. In order that the country be soundly governed, it is important that the king should demonstrate that he has himself under control: this demonstration is manifest when Falstaff is rejected in the final scene of the play. Falstaff had always imagined that one day he would have a free hand, by means of his supposed influence over the Prince.

In *Part I* Hal has already revealed that Falstaff's vision lacked reality: it had always been his intention to reject his 'ill angel'. The Prince's purpose in familiarizing himself with the ways of the wicked and lawless was a self-conscious ploy that he might learn about them, the better to control them when he became king. Despite the appearances, which fooled many, Hal has always been a devotee of order and good government. This is not to say that he did not feel the attraction, as a young man, of the forces of wildness. It is arguable that Shakespeare's presentation of Hal has always been that of a man who, conscious of his destiny, had, in a sense, to conquer those undisciplined forces within himself, in order to assume the mantle of kingship which destiny had thrust upon him. This entailed some self-sacrifice because the king is also a man (with the weaknesses which are inherent in all mankind), but to be a king he cannot be as other men. For this reason, the rejection speech might well be played so that it reveals Hal's regret that things must be as they are – but, in order to become an effective king, he must eschew the undisciplined common humanity, which is represented by the presence of Falstaff. Thus we see at the end of the play that Henry V, in demonstrating self-control, reveals himself ready to exert control over the state, which has been purged of the disruptive elements consequent upon his father's usurpation.

It may also be noted that the country over which Henry V must rule, although 'diseased' (as we have seen), nonetheless has a basic strength and resilience. Gloucestershire may temporarily be under the sway of the incompetent Shallow, but the fundamental fabric of society is sound: the courage of Feeble may for the moment be indeed 'feeble', but it is there to be tapped; prostitution may flourish in some quarters, but honest transactions are still being made at Stamford Fair; the 'hade land' is about to be sown with 'red wheat' and the fruit is abundant in the orchard.

The world of the play

The defeat of the rebel forces by means of the blatant dishonesty which Prince John practises upon the rebels is troubling. It is, of course, in stark contrast with the defeat of the rebels at Shrewsbury, which was accompanied by a sense of chivalry – particularly evident in the farewell tribute paid by the Prince of Wales to his defeated adversary, Hotspur. Prince John's conduct is dishonourable and we may find it hard to excuse it on the grounds that the rebels, too, are men without honour. This is not mere squeamishness: to make the end justify the means is always questionable.

Along with this, we may also consider the view held by some critics that, whatever the self-evident necessity for so doing may be, the rejection of Falstaff by Henry V is again a betrayal. This seems less easy to sustain and derives probably from the hold that Falstaff has exerted over our feelings: it is unlikely that Shakespeare's audience would have felt that Henry had any other option. This does not mean that they would not have regretted the departure of such an attractive character, but wickedness, by its very nature, must seem attractive.

However, it is impossible not to feel that betrayal is an important theme in the play: it seems to arise at every turn. Northumberland betrays his allies and fails to give support to his friends. Henry IV, wrongly as it turns out, feels that Hal has betrayed him – most strongly when he finds that his crown has been taken. The rebels, of course, are betraying their King. Falstaff betrays the trusting Mrs Quickly in not paying his debts and also he betrays the 'friendship' which Shallow feels for him, regarding him merely as wax between his finger-tips. Also, Falstaff betrays the trust put in him by the King in his recruiting methods. Thus, from top to bottom, society is shown to be exploitative and devoid of trust.

If we consider the element of betrayal, along with the prevalence of age and disease which we have already noted, then *Henry IV Part 2* clearly has a dark side to it. Rumour's speech is also important here: it seems to introduce a fickle world in which everything is in a state of flux and in which things rarely seem to turn out as expected. The hopes of Northumberland are dashed in the first scene, when an optimistic report of victory gives way to the truth of defeat. Similarly, the hopes of Falstaff are dashed, together with the expectations of Shallow and co. Sometimes the process works the other way: the King's fears about Hal are not fulfilled, but neither are his hopes to lead a Crusade.

Perhaps the play chronicles the passing of an age: we seem to be in a world where the old chivalric values no longer apply and a new pragmatism is being born.

The characters

King Henry IV

Uneasy lies the head that wears a crown.

For much of the play, Henry IV is presented as a man sick in body, mind and spirit. Such are the fruits of usurpation. Of course, Henry is old and his illness is partly attributable to this simple fact. But it is impossible not to link his symptoms (lack of sleep, for example) with the 'offence' he committed in compassing the crown; hence, too, his stressing to Prince Hal that he will wear the crown by right of succession. Henry IV has been worn out by his endeavours to hold on to what he has gained: his reign has been presented by Shakespeare as one long struggle to maintain his grip on the throne in the teeth of rebellion from erstwhile friends. His griefs have been increased still further by his belief that his son is about to throw away all that he has striven for. It is not surprising that he should say, 'Uneasy lies the head that wears a crown.' He has long-envisaged a crusade to atone for his crime.

Ironically, the King's final defeat of the rebels brings him no joy: by the time he receives the news, his spirits are too low to allow him to take satisfaction from the knowledge. And yet, he dies happy. The reason for this, is, of course, that he dies reconciled with his son. In the play, Henry's feelings about the Prince fluctuate: at one moment he can speak with praise of Hal to Clarence, at the next he has to be comforted by Warwick, so convinced is he that Hal has returned to his old ways. The final straw comes when he discovers that the Prince has removed the crown from his bedchamber. When the Prince returns, the King rounds on him for what he regards as the ultimate betrayal. At this moment, he is convinced that on his death, England will enter a period of misrule. The irony here is that Henry has a genuine concern for the country. Whilst personal ambition has been present in his make-up, it has always coexisted with a disinterested desire to rule well. Thus his castigation of the Prince reveals a personal sense of betrayal (filial ingratitude) and a heartfelt lament at what he believes is about to happen to his beloved England ('O my poor kingdom!'). It is because the Prince is able to assuage both these griefs that he can die happily: a father is reconciled to his son and the king can be confident that his kingdom will be well ruled.

The final irony is that he can also die in 'Jerusalem', although not, as he thought, at the head of a crusade, but in the 'Jerusalem Chamber' at the Palace of Westminster.

The Prince of Wales

The tide of blood in me
Hath proudly flow'd in vanity till now:
Now it doth turn and ebb back to the sea,
Where it shall mingle with the state of floods,
And henceforth flow in formal majesty.

An audience familiar with the Hal of *Henry IV Part 1* would perhaps have been initially surprised to find him still consorting with Poins and Falstaff – but perhaps not disappointed. The surprise is that, in essence, his behaviour seems to take little account of his heroic deeds at the battle of Shrewsbury. We meet him with Poins, in a thoroughly bored, even cynical mood. He laments the company he keeps and shows no little self-disgust: 'Doth it not show vilely in me to desire small beer?' He talks of 'inwardly bleeding' that his father is sick, but this does not prevent him from disguising himself as a waiter, in order to play rather a feeble trick upon Falstaff. There is some merriment in the jest, as we see Falstaff falling into the trap, but the Prince quickly seems to lose interest and contents himself with some half-hearted baiting of his erstwhile fat friend. He leaves blaming himself for profaning 'the precious time'. If we expected anything approaching the high jinks of *Part 1*, then we are disappointed: Falstaff and Hal do not appear together again until the final scene.

Shakespeare does not show us Hal in battle: in a sense he may be said to have 'won his spurs' at Shewsbury. Instead, we focus on the relationship of Hal and his father. The crucial moment occurs when the Prince is moved to take the crown from his father's bedside, put it on his head and retire from the room. When the King awakes he believes that his worst fears have been realized: his son anticipating his death, has unfeelingly snatched the crown prematurely. Of course he is wrong. Before Hal placed the crown on his head his words reveal a young man acutely conscious that, when he does come to wear it, he takes on an awesome responsibility. Indeed, at this moment, ironically, his words echo those of his father: 'O polished perturbation! Golden care! . . .' His defence, before his father, of his preceding actions is very revealing. He returns the crown to his father, thus demonstrating a tact and understanding of the old man's distress. His words are soothing and loyal – and delivered on his knees. There follows a renunciation of his earlier wild days and he speaks of fulfilling a promise which he made to himself – to effect, before 'an incredulous world', a 'noble change'. We are, of course, reminded of the intention which he expressed at the outset of *Henry IV Part 1*, that he would throw off eventually 'this loose behaviour'. Most revealing of all is his assertion that he took the crown and put it on his head 'To try with it as with an enemy'. Some critics take a cynical view of the Prince, and see him here as doing no more than pacifying an old man's distress. It is true that his perfectly judged words do seem to emerge with studied ease, and students of *Part 1* will recollect that the Prince has always shown a facility for playing a part – after all, the entire excursion which he undertook into low-life, as Shakespeare made abundantly clear, was an act played with consummate skill. Nonetheless, his words here do maintain the essential theme of what he said as he contemplated the crown on his father's pillow, and at that time there was no audience (apart from ourselves) – and thus we may assume that he spoke from the heart. After this episode, a reconciliation is achieved between father and son and the old man can die happy in the knowledge that this hard-won crown may be passed safely to his son.

Reconciliation with Henry IV is shortly followed by disavowal of Falstaff. Essentially this is a public occasion. The accusation of heartlessness and insensitivity is hard to sustain. Henry V has no option but to turn away Falstaff – and to make his words effective and have them believed they must be unequivocal and (to Falstaff-lovers) harsh. Much will depend upon how the rejection speech is played. Shakespeare has made it possible for the actor to convey a sense of regret for the necessity of rejecting Falstaff: especially at that point when he grants him an allowance 'for competence of life'. Equally, it would be possible for an actor to render this as though it were a final insult and a dismissive quieting of his own uneasy conscience at what he has to do.

Whatever our feelings about the Prince, it is perhaps difficult to feel much affection for him. Perhaps we are being shown that a king must eschew that element of common humanity which makes a person likable, if he is to perform well in the high office to which destiny has called him. Simply, kings cannot be as ordinary men: their lives should always be dictated by the common good, rather than indulging individual favour. Thus we can understand the absolute necessity for banishing Falstaff, whilst at the same time feeling emotionally outraged by it. The rejection is a studied political act and personal tastes are shown to bow before political necessity. Henry IV is often thought of as a supremely political monarch. There is no reason to believe that his son is any less of a politician; indeed, arguably, the Prince is more subtle, skilful and effective than his father.

The Lord Chief Justice

You are right, justice; and you weigh this well;
Therefore still beat the balance and the sword.

The Lord Chief Justice is important to the play not so much as an interesting character, but more for what he represents. Clearly, he stands opposed to Falstaff, who personifies disorder. The verbal duel in which they engage in Act I Scene 2 is a demonstration of this function: he rebuts everything that Falstaff contends and unequivocally sticks to his guns, 'Your means are very slender and your waste is very great'; 'You have misled the youthful Prince'. Fairmindedly (if mistakenly), he is prepared to grant Falstaff some credit for the supposed valour which he showed at Shrewsbury – but he adamantly refuses the insolent demand that he should lend Falstaff money.

In Act V Scene 2 Hal, as king, hands over to the Lord Chief Justice the symbols of his office – the balance and the sword, together with the injunction that he should employ 'the like bold, just, and impartial spirit/ As you have done 'gainst me'. Thus the King aligns himself with a concept of justice that previously he had seemed to spurn. In submitting his own will to the 'well practised and wise directions' of the Lord Chief Justice, Henry V seems to be saying that no one, not even the king, is above the law. Order in the state demands that all citizens, from the lowest to the highest in rank, should acknowledge adherence to the principles of justice which the Lord Chief Justice represents.

Hal has made a fortunate choice, the Lord Chief Justice has already shown himself to be fearless in his impartiality and it is noteworthy that he is prepared to defend his actions bravely: 'I gave bold way to my authority And did commit you' – this remark, addressed to the new King, indicates his suitability for the office which he has been given.

Prince John

. . . this same young sober-blooded boy.

John is given the responsibility of defeating the Archbishop's forces. He achieves it by means of a trick which leaves us distinctly uneasy: he promises the rebels redress of their grievances, provided that they will disband their army. The Archbishop, taking 'the princely word', agrees to dismiss his forces. Once the rebels begin to disperse John orders the arrest of the rebel leaders and the pursuit of their forces. Execution awaits them. John attributes his victory to God. Of course, we cannot condone rebellion but neither can we feel sympathetic to the cold young man who breaks his word. Political calculation seems to have plumbed the depths: we now appear to be entering an age of pure expediency – for which, it would appear, Prince John is the harbinger. John's treatment of Colevile is devoid of chivalry, and one finds oneself applauding Falstaff's disapproval of 'this same young sober-blooded boy'.

Falstaff

A good wit will make use of anything;
I will turn diseases to commodity.

All other characters in the play pale when set beside Falstaff, yet it is impossible to arrive at a definitive estimate of him. Perhaps we may begin by noting that he is not the man that he was in *Henry IV Part 1*. Critics, with justice, have observed that the zest and wit which was apparent in the earlier play have undergone some diminution. We find it harder to laugh at and excuse his exploitative ways. His sins and follies are thrust before us in a darker light. But we still, in the end, find him irresistible, and, perhaps, there is even a tinge of pathos to be found about him.

Again, we cannot avoid noticing that his ways are essentially disordered – so much so, that he bears a resemblance to the very personification of Vice and Misrule. Our final estimate of the character will depend upon which element we choose to lay stress on in his make-up.

First, let us consider the wicked, disordered Falstaff. The scenes which bring this aspect to the fore are set in Gloucestershire: there is a double exploitation at work here. Obviously, Falstaff is trading for profit on the well-meaning stupidities of Justice Shallow. In this instance, we may feel free to enjoy the comedy: Shallow cannot earn much of our sympathy because he, too, is corrupt and ready to exploit the power of his office; also, the spectacle of Shallow congratulating himself on his performances with various bona robas is ludicrous, and hardly edifying. Where Falstaff must sacrifice our sympathy is in his heartless, mercenary misusing of the 'King's Press'. As the various pathetic specimens of rustic humanity are called before him, Falstaff's gloating over the spoils and his willingness to exploit the courage of the simple-hearted Feeble is hard to excuse. In *Henry IV Part 1* Falstaff made reference to his recruiting methods, as he led his tattered company to battle at Shrewsbury. He had proclaimed the recruits themselves to be mere 'food for powder'. In this play, however, we actually *see* him at work – and the effect is to emphasize the unsavouriness of the process. Our considered judgement of the business must arouse disgust, together with some self-disgust, perhaps, that we find the episode 'funny'. And in this instance, Falstaff lacks the wit to justify his ways. It is worth remembering that to an Elizabethan audience the evil of such methods of recruiting would have been well-recognized.

In *Henry IV Part 1* Falstaff had frequently referred to his youth, vigour and his intention to 'reform'. Not for one moment did we take such asseveration, seriously – nor, for that matter, did Falstaff himself. Remarks on this theme were often delivered with a twinkle in his eye. In *Part 2*, one feels that Falstaff takes himself more seriously. It is as if he really believes some of the legend which has grown up around him after his 'heroism' at Shrewsbury. Certainly, he seems to sense real power – once Prince Hal becomes king. The result is that he is given to a great deal of self-glorification: promising to use his influence to elevate his friends. He struts and plays the *grand seigneur* in Gloucestershire.

The suggestion that Falstaff was growing old is present in *Part 1*. In *Part 2* the ravages of age, decay and disease are much more apparent. His first enquiry (about the condition of his urine) brings to our attention the fact that Falstaff is diseased, and he refers directly to the gout 'which plays the rogue with my great toe'. Furthermore, he is seen consorting with Doll Tearsheet who, it is suggested, is infected with venereal disease. Age is rapidly catching up with Falstaff – even the vigour of his mind which had enabled him wittily to escape from 'difficult' situations in *Part 1*, is absent in *Part 2*: his plea 'No abuse' when he is caught out by the Prince in Act II Scene 4, is feeble. Falstaff sharpens his wits upon Shallow, but he is no match for the Lord Chief Justice.

When Henry comes to reject his former companion our reason tells us that he is right to do so. Falstaff's fantastic belief that the laws of England will be at his command represents the height of his self-delusion, and the audience cannot be surprised at his dismissal from the King's presence. As we have seen, in *Part 2* Shakespeare has taken some care to alienate Falstaff from our sympathies and there are many pointers that the rejection is to come – long before it actually happens. Nonetheless, we should not be human if we did not feel a pang of sorrow when the inevitable happens. Part of the reason for this resides in the power which Falstaff has exerted over our imaginations. Diseased and old he may be, but he is also human. It is this fact, that he encapsulates the follies and vices of the world in which we live, that enables us to feel emotionally attached to him. He sums up all that may be understood by the phrase 'lovable rogue'. True, his roguishness may be closer to villainy in *Part 2* and his treatment of Mrs Quickly is mean-spirited ('Hook on, hook on'), but nevertheless there is a part of us which applauds his praise of sack and his instinctive dislike for the coldness of Prince John, who we may be sure is addicted to thin potations.

Whatever Falstaff's sins, there is no doubt that he creates around himself an atmosphere of good cheer, although the Chief Justice, Prince John and (at the end of the play) Hal, seem immune. We, the audience, of course enjoy him – even his mighty girth seems to radiate an infinite capacity for enjoying himself and causing others to share his enjoyments – 'I am not only witty in myself, but the cause of wit in others.'

Justice Shallow

And now this Vice's dagger is become a squire,
and talks as familiarly of John of Gaunt as if
he had been sworn brother to him.

Justice Shallow is a major source of comedy in the play. He bumbles his way through life in blissful ignorance of his own foolishness. An old man, his high opinion of his own importance is built upon the myth of what he believes he was like when he was young. Like many old men, he lives in the past and continually reminisces about his student days in London, when as an associate of Sir John Falstaff, he earned the nickname of 'mad Shallow'; he is especially proud of his imagined sexual prowess. Falstaff reveals that Shallow's past, in reality, amounted to little or nothing; every third word which he speaks is a lie, and Shallow was chiefly famous for his fantastic thinness. Like some of the other characters in the play, Shallow is aptly named.

Along with the basic foolishness of Shallow there goes a certain country shrewdness; thus in the middle of his 'meditation' on the certainty of death, he can suddenly interrupt himself with the inapposite remark, 'How a good yoke of bullocks at Stamford fair?' He is also clever enough to perceive that by latching himself on to Falstaff he may achieve some advancement. This seeking after the main chance makes him easy meat for Falstaff, who contemptuously regards him as wax between his finger-tips. His toadying to Falstaff reveals Shallow in a less attractive light: he is prepared to go along with Sir John's methods of recruiting. He is the personification of the corrupt petty official who is prepared to bend the law at the behest of his serving-man, Davy. It is perhaps a point in Shallow's favour that even he is irritated by the inane Pistol. We can afford to laugh wholeheartedly at Shallow: he is harmless, and Shakespeare clearly enjoys him and expects us to do likewise.

Pistol

A rag-bag of misquotations from bombastic plays, ludicrous pretensions to soldiership and fearsomeness, Pistol is one of the most gloriously comic of Shakespeare's minor creations. No one can put up with him for very long: Mrs Quickly cannot abide his swaggering and Falstaff is moved to thrust him downstairs. His moment of glory comes when it is given to him to announce the death of Henry IV and the accession of Henry V – a piece of news that he takes pleasure in delivering at inordinate length.

Mrs Quickly

As Hostess of the Boar's Head tavern, Mrs Quickly has suffered at the hands of Falstaff, who owes her money. At the beginning of the play she is apparently prepared to call in the bailiffs to obtain repayment, but Falstaff is not long in worming his way back into her favour. We should not lose sight of the fact that she is a brothel-keeper, but she endears herself to us by her basic good-heartedness and her tendency to muddle her words into the most fantastic malapropisms. We are told that a man has died in suspicious circumstances under her roof, but not even this can prevent us from feeling outraged when she is brutally hauled off to prison at the end of the play.

Doll Tearsheet

A whore and Sir John's paramour, Doll is chiefly remarkable for the foulness of her utterances and her willingness to bear the mighty Sir John as her lover. The spectacle of her embracing Falstaff may be ludicrous, disgusting or pathetic, according to taste.

Silence

Silence (his character is suggested by his name) is Shallow's fellow justice in Gloucestershire. His dramatic function is to act as a comic foil to Shallow, by whom he is constantly patronized. Oddly enough, he belies his name in Act V Scene 3, when, to great comic effect, he bursts into tipsy song.

The Archbishop of York

The spectacle of an Archbishop in arms against the King, dignifying rebellion with the name of God, is deeply offensive and represents the disorder which has come to haunt the reign of Henry IV. The Archbishop, together with the other rebels, seems to have little pretext for his revolt, other than exploitation for personal ends of the weakness of the King and the general unrest in the country. There is some talk of ill-defined 'grievances', but the overriding motivation for all the rebels seems to be merely a hatred of the King. The rebellion is ill-founded and the Archbishop's willingness to trust the word of Prince John springs essentially from an assessment of the comparative weakness of his forces.

Northumberland

Northumberland is shown to be sick, old and treacherous. At the beginning, we are told that he was 'crafty-sick' and hence avoided commitment at the Battle of Shrewsbury. At the request of his wife and daughter-in-law, he leaves the Archbishop in the lurch and retires to the relative safety of Scotland. The last we hear of him is that he has been defeated by the Sheriff of York.

Style

Verse

For the most part Shakespeare adheres to the convention that the nobility speak in verse, whereas the lower orders speak in prose. The blank verse in *Henry IV Part 2* is not generally moving or memorable. The speeches of the rebels, reflecting perhaps the nature of their cause, are full of sound and fury but signify little. Lord Bardolph's speech ('When we mean to build. . .') in Act I Scene 3 is memorable and clever, but can hardly be said to carry with it a sense of the dramatic situation in which it is set: essentially, it remains a set-piece which might derive from any one of the rebels, rather than being stamped with the personality of the speaker.

Shakespeare does, on other occasions, give his characters verse which matches their natures: Prince John, for example, speaks verse of stiff formality which matches his sober character. The King, in his long speech on his inability to sleep (Act III Scene 1), is given verse which is particularly rich in imagery as he contemplates those who are granted the gift of repose, which is denied to him. His thoughts are seen to wander restlessly amidst the humble, both on land and sea: here the rhythms of sleep and the soft, lulling sound of the words contrast strongly with his agitated questioning of 'partial sleep' itself, with which the speech concludes. The verse vividly enacts in sound the sense of what is being described. The Prince's speech as he confronts the crown in Act IV Scene 5, which is on much the same theme, whilst it shows a kinship between father and son, is much calmer in tone and is clearly the utterance of a man who is far surer of himself. When Hal becomes king, his words become formal and are spoken with authority (notably to the Lord Chief Justice in Act V Scene 2 – 'You are right, Justice, and you weigh this well. . .'). Much the same tone of formality is present when he comes to reject Falstaff, although there is a notable break in the rigidities of the rhythm, when he drops the imperiousness, to speak more humanely to Falstaff – the 'thees' and 'thous' now become 'yous', the sounds are softer and there is more 'flow' in what he says: the King has become gentle.

In a lighter vein, Shakespeare has some fun with his character Pistol, who speaks verse almost entirely derived from the 'rant tragedies' which enjoyed a vogue in Shakespeare's day.

Prose

If the verse of the play is somewhat unyielding, there are many glories in the prose. Here Shakespeare demonstrates his mastery of nuance and tone. We find the comic vituperation of Doll Tearsheet, who is able to pile insult upon obscenity and yet, almost in the same breath, she changes to the sentimental utterances of the practised whore: 'I love thee better than I love e'er a scurvy young boy of them all.' We find the joyous malapropisms of Mrs Quickly and the reminiscences and non-sequiturs of the aged Shallow, who is approaching senility – yet retains enough shrewdness to interject the pointed and sharp: 'A colour that I fear you will die in, Sir John.'

Falstaff's praise of 'sherris-sack' is a masterpiece of prose; it begins with a leisurely, insolent sneering at 'these demure boys' who favour 'thin drink', accelerates as it describes the supposed effects of the sack, 'quick, forgetive, full of nimble and fiery and delectable shapes'. Next we hear the enhancing attributes of the drink in terms of extreme hyperbole, as Falstaff employs military metaphor, 'the heart, who, great and puffed up with his retinue, doth any deed of courage, and this valour comes of sherris'. The speech concludes on a climactic, absurd note before returning to the theme with which it began: 'If I had a thousand sons, the first humane principle I would teach them should be to forswear thin potations and to addict themselves to sack'. Here, as elsewhere, Shakespeare has contrived, in the writing of an extremely artful speech, to convey a sense of immediacy: the illusion is to make the listener suppose that Falstaff is making it up as he goes along.

Imagery

Imagery provides emotional and intellectual illumination on characters, themes and situations in the plays. The prevailing mood of a play is often pointed up by repeated or iterative images.

Inescapably, for example, we notice that there is a constant reference to the effects of age and disease in the play: Falstaff is described as being 'withered elder' with his 'poll clawed like a parrot'; the Lord Chief Justice describes Falstaff 'as a candle, the better part burnt out'. These and many other such images contrive to present Falstaff as old and sometimes disgusting, 'a globe of sinful continents'. It is not only Falstaff who is diseased and aged: the King himself refers to his 'bare withered trunk' (cf. Falstaff, 'a dead elm'); Northumberland, although 'crafty-sick' is first seen swathed in bandages and supported by a crutch – a powerful visual image of impotence and decay.

Another frequent motif in the imagery suggests that the diseases which afflict the characters are the result of an excess of appetite. This is particularly evident with Falstaff, whose bloated figure ('surfeit-swelled'), is the result of a lifetime's 'gormandizing'. At one point in the play, the Archbishop says, 'We are all diseased,/ And with our surfeiting and wanton hours/ Have brought ourselves into a burning fever, / And must bleed for it.' Thus it may be inferred that there is a parallel between Falstaff's self-indulgence and the appetite for power which has infected the rebels as it once infected the King, who seized the crown. Man must of necessity learn to control his appetites if he, or the State, is to survive.

The prevalence of 'disease imagery' together with the presence of so many aged and ailing characters makes a powerful contribution to the overall sombre tone of the play.

General questions

1 'False-report befools everyone.' (A.P. Rossiter). Discuss this theme in *Henry IV Part 2*.

Outline of points to cover in your answer

(a) *Introduction:*
Rumour's speech: introduces the idea of false-report. Immediately exemplified in the first scene: Northumberland receives false-report of victory at Shrewsbury. Hope shakily rebuilt on report of Archbishop in arms – his strength proves to be over-estimated.

(b) *Any other relevant examples?*

- Falstaff still able to capitalize on the reputation he enjoys for valour at Shrewsbury. Climaxed by capitulation of Coleville at Gaultree. John and Chief Justice are sceptics.
- Shallow believes Falstaff's estimate of himself as the Prince's friend and mentor. Shallow himself is given to believing his 'mad Shallow' fabrication. Falstaff reveals the truth about Shallow's past.
- After stating his faith in his son, Henry IV relapses into an admittedly temporary belief that Hal has reverted to his old ways – on the strength of a false-report from Clarence.
- The rebels put their faith in the arrival of Northumberland who betrays their trust; they also believe that John will grant them pardon and redress – they are wrong.
- Falstaff arrives in London expecting favours from the new King – his hopes are rudely shattered.

(c) *Thus:*
It is true that the play exemplifies the divergence between what appears to be true and the reality of things. The appearances are frequently based upon false-reports of the various situations. Also the situations themselves seem sometimes to betoken hopes which turn out to have been misplaced.

Only in the case of Henry IV (believing his son to have

reverted to his former ways) is the reality more fortunate than the illusion.

Final estimate:
We see that the play presents a world in which expectations frequently prove false – in this sense the play presents the fickleness of the times. Hal is believed to be wild; the reality is otherwise. Yet on other occasions hopes of success prove false. There seems no particular reason for us to put our faith in anything that appears to be true – the chances are that we shall be proved wrong, one way or another – like so many of the characters in the play. The safest course would seem to be a healthy scepticism.

2 What is the relevance of the Induction to the rest of the play?
3 'A play permeated with a feeling of sickness, age and death.' Discuss.
4 Compare and contrast the significance and impact of the town and country scenes.
5 How do you think that Shakespeare intends we should regard the rebels and their cause?
6 What relationship do you find between the 'Falstaff-plot' and the 'political-plot'?
7 How justified was Henry in rejecting Falstaff?
8 Discuss the significance of the Lord Chief Justice.
9 'A play without a hero.' How far do you agree?
10 Why do you think that Shakespeare found it necessary to write an Epilogue?
11 'Its glories are to be found in the prose rather than in the verse.' Discuss this view with reference to the play's language.
12 'We may admire the Prince, but we cannot like him.' Discuss.
13 Show how Shakespeare presents Henry IV as a king who is haunted by his past.
14 Elucidate the significance of the scene in which the Prince is reconciled with his father.
15 'A play full of treachery.' Comment.
16 Discuss the artistry in Shakespeare's presentation of the character of Justice Shallow.
17 'In *Henry IV Part 2* we find more darkness than light.' How far do you agree?
18 Discuss the theme of 'law and order' in the play.

19 Show how the imagery reflects some of the major preoccupations of the play.

20 Estimate the importance of Prince John with reference to the play as a whole.

Further reading

The Arden Shakespeare: Henry IV, Part 2, ed. A. R. Humphreys (Methuen, 1966).

The Signet Classic: Henry IV, Part 2, ed. N. N. Holland (NAL, 1965).

Casebook series: Henry IV, Parts 1 & 2, ed. G. K. Hunter (Macmillan, 1970).

The Cease of Majesty, M. M. Reese (Arnold, 1961).

The Elizabethan World Picture, E. M. W. Tillyard (Penguin, 1972).

Shakespeare's History Plays, E. M. W. Tillyard (Chatto, 1980).

Shakespeare from Richard II to Henry V, D. A. Traversi (Hollis & Carter, 1958).

Shakespeare's Doctrine of Nature, J. A. Danby (Faber & Faber, 1949).

Pan study aids Titles published in the Brodie's Notes series

W. H. Auden Selected Poetry

Jane Austen Emma Mansfield Park Northanger Abbey Persuasion Pride and Prejudice

Anthologies of Poetry Ten Twentieth Century Poets The Poet's Tale The Metaphysical Poets

Samuel Beckett Waiting for Godot

Arnold Bennett The Old Wives' Tale

William Blake Songs of Innocence and Experience

Robert Bolt A Man for All Seasons

Harold Brighouse Hobson's Choice

Charlotte Brontë Jane Eyre

Emily Brontë Wuthering Heights

Robert Browning Selected Poetry

John Bunyan The Pilgrim's Progress

Geoffrey Chaucer (parallel texts editions) The Franklin's Tale The Knight's Tale The Miller's Tale The Nun's Priest's Tale The Pardoner's Tale Prologue to the Canterbury Tales The Wife of Bath's Tale

Richard Church Over the Bridge

John Clare Selected Poetry and Prose

Samuel Taylor Coleridge Selected Poetry and Prose

Wilkie Collins The Woman in White

William Congreve The Way of the World

Joseph Conrad The Nigger of the Narcissus & Youth The Secret Agent

Charles Dickens Bleak House David Copperfield Dombey and Son Great Expectations Hard Times Little Dorrit Oliver Twist Our Mutual Friend A Tale of Two Cities

Gerald Durrell My Family and Other Animals

George Eliot Middlemarch The Mill on the Floss Silas Marner

T. S. Eliot Murder in the Cathedral Selected Poems

J. G. Farrell The Siege of Krishnapur

Henry Fielding Joseph Andrews

F. Scott Fitzgerald The Great Gatsby

E. M. Forster Howards End A Passage to India
Where Angels Fear to Tread

William Golding Lord of the Flies The Spire

Oliver Goldsmith Two Plays of Goldsmith: She Stoops to Conquer; The Good Natured Man

Graham Greene Brighton Rock The Power and the Glory
The Quiet American

Thom Gunn and Ted Hughes Selected Poems

Thomas Hardy Chosen Poems of Thomas Hardy
Far from the Madding Crowd Jude the Obscure
The Mayor of Casterbridge Return of the Native
Tess of the d'Urbervilles The Trumpet-Major

L. P. Hartley The Go-Between The Shrimp and the Anemone

Joseph Heller Catch-22

Ernest Hemingway For Whom the Bell Tolls
The Old Man and the Sea

Barry Hines A Kestrel for a Knave

Gerard Manley Hopkins Poetry and Prose of Gerard Manley Hopkins

Aldous Huxley Brave New World

Henry James Washington Square

Ben Jonson The Alchemist Volpone

James Joyce A Portrait of the Artist as a Young Man Dubliners

John Keats Selected Poems and Letters of John Keats

Ken Kesey One Flew over the Cuckoo's Nest

Rudyard Kipling Kim

D. H. Lawrence The Rainbow Selected Tales Sons and Lovers

Harper Lee To Kill a Mockingbird

Laurie Lee As I Walked out One Midsummer Morning
Cider with Rosie

Thomas Mann Death in Venice & Tonio Kröger

Christopher Marlowe Doctor Faustus Edward the Second

W. Somerset Maugham Of Human Bondage

Gavin Maxwell Ring of Bright Water

Thomas Middleton The Changeling

Arthur Miller The Crucible Death of a Salesman

John Milton A Choice of Milton's Verse Comus and Samson Agonistes Paradise Lost I, II

Sean O'Casey Juno and the Paycock
The Shadow of a Gunman and the Plough and the Stars

George Orwell Animal Farm 1984

John Osborne Luther

Alexander Pope Selected Poetry

J. B. Priestley An Inspector Calls

Siegfried Sassoon Memoirs of a Fox-Hunting Man

Peter Shaffer The Royal Hunt of the Sun

William Shakespeare Antony and Cleopatra As You Like It Coriolanus Hamlet Henry IV (Part I) Henry IV (Part II) Henry V Julius Caesar King Lear Love's Labour's Lost Macbeth Measure for Measure The Merchant of Venice A Midsummer Night's Dream Much Ado about Nothing Othello Richard II Richard III Romeo and Juliet The Sonnets The Taming of the Shrew The Tempest Twelfth Night The Winter's Tale

G. B. Shaw Arms and the Man
Caesar and Cleopatra The Doctor's Dilemma Pygmalion Saint Joan

Richard Sheridan Plays of Sheridan: The Rivals; The Critic; The School for Scandal

John Steinbeck The Grapes of Wrath Of Mice and Men & The Pearl

Tom Stoppard Rosencrantz and Guildenstern are Dead

J. M. Synge The Playboy of the Western World

Jonathan Swift Gulliver's Travels

Alfred Tennyson Selected Poetry

William Thackeray Vanity Fair

Flora Thompson Lark Rise to Candleford

Dylan Thomas Under Milk Wood

Anthony Trollope Barchester Towers

Mark Twain Huckleberry Finn

Keith Waterhouse Billy Liar

Evelyn Waugh Decline and Fall Scoop

H. G. Wells The History of Mr Polly The War of the Worlds

John Webster The Duchess of Malfi The White Devil

Oscar Wilde The Importance of Being Earnest

Virginia Woolf To the Lighthouse

William Wordsworth The Prelude (Books 1, 2)

William Wycherley The Country Wife

John Wyndham The Chrysalids

W. B. Yeats Selected Poetry

Pan study aids

Published jointly by Heinemann Educational Books and Pan Books

Pan Study Aids is a major new series developed to help school and college students prepare for examinations. All the authors are experienced teachers/examiners at O level, School Certificate and equivalent examinations and authors of textbooks used in schools and colleges worldwide

Each volume in the series:

- explains its subject and covers clearly and concisely and with excellent illustrations the essential points of the syllabus, drawing attention to common areas of difficulty and to areas which carry most marks in the exam
- gives guidance on how to plan revision, and prepare for the exam, outlining what examiners are looking for
- provides practice by including typical exam questions and exercises

Titles available: Physics, Chemistry, Maths, Human Biology, English Language, Geography 1 & 2, Economics, Commerce, Accounts and Book-keeping, British Government and Politics, History 1 & 2, Effective Study Skills, French, German, Spanish, Sociology

Pan Study Aids Check Tests
Books of multiple-choice questions designed specifically to help students revise and prepare for O level and similar exams. Use the magic marker to check your answer – at the end of each question write your answer in one box, then rub over the check box and the correct answer will be revealed.

Each book sets questions of exactly the same format and style as those of the examining boards. These provide a comprehensive revision course, check your knowledge and revision progress, and give essential practice in the completion of multiple-choice questions.

Edward Wakeling
Check Test Maths
By the head of maths/computer studies at Stopsley High School in Luton and examiner for maths for the East Anglia CSE Board.

Colin Clegg
Check Test Biology
The author is lecturer in biology at Bournemouth and Poole College of Further Education and author of *Advanced Biology* in the Pan Study Aids series.

John Clarke
Check Test Chemistry
By the head of science at Alleyn's School in London, also a reviser for JMB O and A level chemistry and author of *Teach Yourself Chemistry.*

J. J. Wellington
Check Test Physics
The author is lecturer in education (physics and computer studies) at the division of education of Sheffield University, formerly head of physics at Daneford Comprehensive School, Bethnal Green, London.

Use the magic marker to check your answers!

Pan Literature Guides

Marguerite Alexander
An Introduction to Shakespeare and his Contemporaries
From the mid-sixteenth century to the closing of the theatres in 1642, English drama proved the finest flowering of the English renaissance. Marguerite Alexander's *Literature Guide* examines the themes and development of Elizabethan and Jacobean drama, going on to explore the social conditions and literary and folk traditions that combined to produce the period's unique poetry and drama.

John Cargill Thompson
An Introduction to British Drama 1660–1900
John Cargill Thompson's Literature Guide pinpoints fifty major landmarks of dramatic writing from the reopening of the theatres under the Stuart kings, the Restoration plays, through the sophisticated entertainments of Goldsmith and Sheridan, to the stages of Victorian England where Wilde and Pinero saw the curtain fall on the last act of the nineteenth century.

Benedict Nightingale
An Introduction to Fifty Modern British Plays
The last eighty years have seen a constant flow of fine theatre across the English-speaking stage – from the Edwardian finale of Shaw and Maugham, through the *entr'acte* of Coward and Priestley, to the new vision of the 1950s and the radical creativity of the last decade. Benedict Nightingale takes fifty important and influential plays, examining each in the context of the wider output of the playwright, and providing a lively and comprehensive survey of the drama of our times.

Reference, language and information

☐	**The Story of Language**	C. L. Barber	£2.50p
☐	**North-South**	Brandt Commission	£2.50p
☐	**Test Your IQ**	Butler and Pirie	£1.50p
☐	**Writing English**	D. J. Collinson	£1.50p
☐	**Illustrating Computers**	Colin Day and Donald Alcock	£1.95p
☐	**Dictionary of Famous Quotations**	Robin Hyman	£2.95p
☐	**Militant Islam**	Godfrey Jansen	£1.50p
☐	**The War Atlas**	Michael Kidron and Dan Smith	£5.95p
☐	**Practical Statistics**	R. Langley	£1.95p
☐	**How to Study**	H. Maddox	£1.95p
☐	**The Limits to Growth**	D. H. Meadows et al.	£2.50p
☐	**Your Guide to the Law**	ed. Michael Molyneux	£3.95p
☐	**Ogilvy on Advertising**	David Ogilvy	£6.95p
☐	**Common Security**	Palme Commission	£1.95p
☐	**The Modern Crossword Dictionary**	Norman Pulsford	£3.50p
☐	**A Guide to Saving and Investment**	James Rowlatt	£2.95p
☐	**Career Choice**	Audrey Segal	£3.95p
☐	**Logic and its Limits**	Patrick Shaw	£2.95p
☐	**Names for Boys and Girls**	L. Sleigh and C. Johnson	£1.95p
☐	**Straight and Crooked Thinking**	R. H. Thouless	£1.95p
☐	**Money Matters**	Harriet Wilson	£1.75p
☐	**Dictionary of Earth Sciences**		£2.95p
☐	**Dictionary of Physical Sciences**		£2.95p